Travel with a Pen

Travel with a Pen

Glenn Martin

G.P. Martin Publishing

Published 2023 by G.P. Martin Publishing
Website: www.glennmartin.com.au
Contact: info@glennmartin.com.au

Book layout and cover design by the author
Typeset in Sitka 11 pt
Printed by Lulu.com

Cover images and design by the author.
Front cover: Mount Wellington (kunanyi), Hobart.
Back cover: Hastings Caves (Newdegate Cave).

ISBN: 978 0 6488433 9 9 (pbk.)

NATIONAL
LIBRARY
OF AUSTRALIA

A catalogue record for this
book is available from the
National Library of Australia

I am flying to Hobart (from Sydney) for a twelve-day visit. In Tasmania, I will use buses as my only transport apart from my feet. I will spend most of my time in Hobart. I am attending my graduation from the University of Tasmania in a Diploma of Family History, then travelling to Oatlands (in the midlands) to search for clues to my great great grandmother's presence there (as a convict) in 1850. And I will visit places I haven't seen before.

Life is a series of stories, intricately interwoven. I write the stories as I go.

Sunday 20 Aug 2023

I was booked on Virgin Airlines, Sydney to Hobart, leaving 10:10 am, Sunday morning. A blue sky, a clear day, crisp. I booked the airport shuttle bus and it arrived on time at 7:30 am, a modern large van. It had two other passengers, a couple from Castle Hill who were returning to New Zealand – with one suitcase! All smooth, and I arrived early at the airport.

I organised myself, printed everything out, but it's still hard to figure out what you have to do. I still have to check in one suitcase. They had helper-persons, so I didn't try, I just asked for help. This looks more legitimate as I get older. I got to the departure gate and had time to read for an hour.

I was in the ninth row in the plane, window seat and no one beside me. A German lady was in the aisle seat with her husband sitting directly behind her. Why? I don't know. So many things every day we don't know. The plane was quite full. Were they holiday-makers, people returning home, Australians, Asians, British tourists travelling in the off-season? None of the above or all of the above.

I like the window seat because, if you're flying, wouldn't you want to see where you are going? Wouldn't you like to see the sky, and the ground, and the clouds, and the sea? It's hard to see where the country goes, because the clouds just disappear into the distance and there is no horizon.

When we were going across Victoria, there were lots of forests and mountains, and often just the single thread of a road passing through. Most people live in cities, but the mountains are still there. I saw the line of the beaches marking the southern coast of Victoria, and then there was just water and patches of clouds. Not rough; no shipwrecks today.

I saw the line of beaches marking the northern coast of Tasmania. There was an inlet that could have been the Tamar River that goes down to Launceston. We flew down the east coast to

1

Hobart. At times, the sea was so clear that it could have been glass, deep, blue glass. At other times, the surface was rippled all over. No great waves, no turbulence, just a surface shimmer in different shades of blue.

We got to Hobart just after noon. Getting luggage was slow, because several planes arrived at about the same time. But of course, in time it all works out. People find their bags and leave – old people, people with children, who are invariably excited, and the occasional solo traveller, like me.

I was hoping there would be a bus out front that would take passengers who had not booked a seat, and there was. Twenty dollars for the trip. The driver seemed to decide to leave when he thought he had enough people. He took me to a bus stop just one block from the Hotel Astor. He also stopped outside the Grand Chancellor Hotel, where I have to go tomorrow to sort out my graduation gear.

It was about 1:30 pm when I arrived near the Hotel Astor. I wasn't booked to arrive until 3:00 pm, and I thought maybe they don't man the desk outside of the set hours. But my bags were heavy: 12.5 kg for the suitcase, and 5.7 kg for the backpack. So, I went in, left my suitcase on the ground floor and walked up to Level One where reception is.

There was no one at reception, as expected, but there was a lady sitting in the loungeroom, and she told me to ring the phone number on the sign on the reception desk, and Tilly or Neil would come down. I am positive this same lady was sitting just there the last time I was here, around four years ago, and she said exactly the same thing. She had a magazine on the table in front of her, and she was doing a crossword. And yes, last time she was doing the same thing.

It was Neil who came down, and it was the same Neil who had been here four years ago, and he said, "Haven't you stayed here before?" Indeed I had.

He walked downstairs and put my suitcase into the lift that carries baggage only. Up it came, all by itself. Then I noticed, just near the lift door, an exhibit. It looked like a church building, about 900 mm high, with spires and dark wood, except that there were vertical steel bars instead of walls. It sat on a square table made of similar dark wood, nicely turned. I had to ask two questions: Was that there before? And, what is it?

I evidently have a good memory, because Neil told me that Tilly had only acquired it recently at an auction house in Hobart. It was a bird cage! Neil was pleased that I had noticed, and pleased that I liked it.

He said I had a choice of two rooms, and he showed me. The first room was large, and it had beautiful old wooden furniture. The other room was nice, but dark. I'm sure this was the room I stayed in last time. I liked the first room; it had more light, and nicer furniture. It also had a small shower in the corner, which doesn't matter a lot, because there is a bathroom across the corridor, and also, there don't seem to be many people staying here at the moment.

After I had shed the load of my bags, I went out, because I was hungry. I promised myself that I wouldn't just do the same things I did last time, but there are four boats down at the harbour that were floating seafood cafes, so I thought that might be worth repeating. I ordered scallops and chips, simple fare. It was nice enough – not gourmet, but nice for a hungry man. Oh, and the music: it sounded like The Beatles from around 1964 – those songs from their early albums, but they sounded like different versions, as if Paul Macartney or George Martin had been trawling through the archives and found them. So that was rather pleasant and evocative.

One thing I hadn't done on my previous travels was to go to the Tasmanian Museum and Art Gallery, so I found it and went there. I only had an hour until they closed, but it's close enough, and if I want to come back tomorrow, I will. It was, as museums tend to be, interesting, but I won't enumerate all the exhibits. There were some exhibits based around Charles Dickens, because he visited Australia, and Hobart. He also came to Sydney, and there is a statue of him there – in Centennial Park, I think. (Yes; it was created in 1891.)

The emphasis in the exhibition was on his books. Apparently, when he was releasing *Oliver Twist* in serial form, for the English and American markets, a printing press in Hobart was printing the articles/stories and distributing them locally. It's nice to hear a good book story. I should note that opposite the Hotel Astor is a building that has "Bookbinder" carved into its stonework. Maybe they printed the Dickens serials!

I went into one room that had many nineteenth-century portraits on the walls. What took my interest were two longish tables in the middle of the room. They were covered with black velvet. I wondered why you would put something on exhibit but then cover it up. Usually if there is something you have to do, there are instructions everywhere, but there was not a word in sight. So, I ignored them at first.

When I was walking around the room, I found myself looking at the tables from the other side, and I realised there was a dowel through the edge of the velvet. Obviously, this was to keep the edge down, but conversely, it meant you could pick the edge up. So I did. What I found were some very old books underneath, early copies of novels by Charles Dickens. One of them was *Great Expectations*. Another cover revealed a letter written by Charles Dickens. Hidden treasures!

After the museum, I wandered down to the wharves. I know I said I would not spend all my time revisiting things I saw last time, but I was very close to the statues of the female convicts, so I went to see them. I had taken photos before, but I realised that to be comprehensive, I should take photos of the base of each statue, because the names of some of the women were written in the brass that the statues stood on, and the names of some of the ships that brought them. I didn't find Sarah Crosby, my great great grandmother, or the *St Vincent*, the ship that brought her here in April 1850.

There was no reason for the history buffs to take notice of Sarah. She didn't bring a child with her from England or Ireland, as some of the women did. She didn't figure in the public history of Tasmania; she married Edward Lewis in 1853, and by 1857 they had left the state for New South Wales, never to return.

By the time she died (1897), her children were trying to eliminate any mention of Tasmania, because of its convict associations. On her death certificate, her eldest daughter changed many of the details of her mother's life. She stated that her mother was born in Ireland (true), married Edward Lewis in Ireland(false!), and in Australia she had lived in Victoria and New South Wales, but never in Tasmania (Victoria seems to have been substituted for Tasmania).

Sarah didn't distinguish herself by her exploits. Her main misdemeanour was to have a child in 1851 to an unnamed father, a child that we presume died, but the baby's death is not recorded. Many convict women had babies to unnamed fathers, and many babies died without record.

I walked to where the Salamanca markets are held, which is on Saturdays, and had a coffee in the dying sun. It was indeed a temperate day, with no ice in the air. People were venturing forth in tee-shirts, although I was comfortable in my flannelette shirt and light jacket. After coffee, I found a walkway between the shops called Kelly's Stairs, and walked up, because it went to Battery Point, and I will be staying there later this week, at the Shipwrights Arms Hotel. It was a steep staircase and very old.

When I got to the top, all the houses in the street were very old and charming. They were neat and lovely. One garden had lots of flowers, which I think is quite a feat in the middle of winter in Tasmania. This area has clearly become genteel. Some of the houses had memorial plaques on them. Some were described as "gentleman's residences". I think that is an exquisite concept, but I struggle to visualise what it is supposed to be.

Is it a single man with servants? Is it a man with no apparent trade or occupation? Is it an important man who happens to be not married? Or may he still be married? One of them was certainly important. He built the house in about 1903, and he is credited with being the main architect of the Australian Constitution: Andrew Inglis Clark.

The view from Battery Point is wonderful, looking down onto the Derwent River. After that I walked back through Prince's Park to Salamanca. It was Sunday afternoon, and a lady was singing at one of the pubs, in the outside area, the footpath, or the front courtyard. Popular songs from the eighties. Solo with an acoustic guitar.

Then I walked up to St David's Park. It is covered with mature trees and numerous memorial statues. Apart from this it has a corridor of stone walls that have gravestones affixed to them. They were taken from a cemetery that gave way to city progress.

Most of the gravestones are from the 1800s, especially the early part of the century, the early days of Hobart. I just like reading the names and dates, and the messages people offer up for their deceased relatives. There were many children who died. One child died two weeks after the family arrived in Hobart from England. There was one family called Lewis (as per my great great grandfather, Edward Lewis), but the gravestone stated they were from a different part of England from Edward, who came from Essex.

Mentioning this reminds me that I have not found Edward's death certificate or grave. He lived in Sydney for much of his life. Perhaps he lived in Newcastle for a few years, but then the trail goes cold. I think he died around the same time as Sarah – 1897, but all I have is stray clues, no clear conclusion. And I certainly won't find anything useful about his death in Tasmania.

Part of my purpose in coming to Tasmania this time is to go to Oatlands, because it seems that when Sarah first arrived in Van Diemen's Land as a convict, she was sent to Oatlands to work as a servant at an inn. Her employer was Charles Sutton. Oatlands is on the road north from Hobart, heading towards Launceston.

I arrived back at the Hotel Astor around 4:30 pm. In bourgeois terms, this was for an afternoon rest before I went out to find dinner. Given that it is Sunday and it is winter in Hobart, it may take some deft hunting to find dinner.

I like my old-fashioned room. It does not have a television. If you want to watch television, you can walk down to the loungeroom where the lady does her crossword. However, wouldn't it be interesting just to not have television for a couple of weeks?

On my way to find dinner, I walked up the road past the Church of St Joseph's, built in 1843 of sandstone. This was the church where Sarah Crosby and Edward Lewis got married in March 1853. Imagine that! At the time, they lived two blocks away, in Watchorn Street. There is nothing left in Watchorn Street from the old days. It is all car parks, garages, a modern apartment building, and the side wall of the Odeon, an old-fashioned cinema. It's just a short street. Although I vowed not to repeat things I had done before, I couldn't resist walking up the street. I consider it devotion, homage to the ancestors.

Next month, the Odeon will feature a show called "Natural Body Builders". I saw a body builders show on an Indian movie. It was quite a spectacle, and possibly the movie did not even do it justice.

There were not many restaurants open, and I don't eat meat, so I avoid some places. I suspect people get food delivered home. That seems to be the way of it these days. What I was not prepared for, however, was the modernisation of food-ordering within the restaurant. I went into one and was met, not with a person, but with a sign with a QR code on it, saying "Scan this to see the menu". I walked into the restaurant and there was only one table where there were people. But there were no staff to be seen. I walked down to the desk at the back, and again I was met with the QR code and no staff.

I did not want to order my meal by clicking on a QR code and looking at my phone. I wanted a human to interface with me, with words and maybe even a smile or an effort. I walked out of this restaurant. At least I didn't upset any humans by doing so. I eventually went into an Asian restaurant that had humans in it.

However, when I sat down, the waiter (a human) came and handed me a menu with a small piece of paper on it that had a QR code on it. He motioned to it.

I said, "I do not wish to do that. I wish to order a meal from you. Can I do that?" I made an effort not to reduce my voice to a mechanical monotone.

He seemed a little disappointed, as if he had a new toy to share and I didn't want to play with it, but he brought me a traditional colourful, glossy menu and I soon found a choice that I thought would be okay. I got my meal, which was quite satisfactory, and then a group of young people came in and sat nearby. I watched their behaviour. I wondered if the young people realised that they were being studied, anthropological-style.

They all pulled out their phones and started looking at them. I could see the QR codes scattered around the table. They seemed to be quite happy doing this. And the waiter stood back, not interfering with the process. On the other hand, nor did they seem to need help or advice. The message about their order seemed to be communicated without words, and before long, the waiter came back with meals for them. But I did not wish to do that.

I was rather torn in eating my meal. It was brought in its own bowl, and it was boiling rapidly upon delivery. I was warned by the waiter that it was hot. So, I could not eat fast; I had to wait for it to cool. However, I couldn't stand the music. It was Asian disco, rapid beat, soaring voices that were uniformly emotionless, and…. And nothing, just over and over, as if they were products of AI. I almost hoped they were. I had to remind myself that the food tasted quite okay.

After I left, I walked up the street past the old Post Office sandstone building, and three girls walked past me and crossed the street. There were charged up as if they were intent on having "a good night". They started banging on the bars of a shutter door and yelling. I suppose it made sense to them. There was nothing sinister about it, it was just a lark on a cold night. By this time, I was walking past a bus stop and some people were waiting there for a bus.

A young man who looked rather scruffy started commenting on them audibly, saying they should grow up. I realised this was for the benefit of his son, who was about nine. He was trying to show he was a good parent. So much is packed into every moment when you walk around a city.

What had initially interested me in the girls was that I thought we were in the next street, where Hadley's Hotel is located. I had taken note of this place last time I was in town, because it would have been a classy place in the 1930s, and it still preserves something of that aura. The hotel turned up in a book I read recently, an autobiography by Alanna Hill (*Butterfly on a Pin*), a Tasmanian girl who became a famous international fashion designer. In her book, as a teenager living in Hobart, she and her friends got dressed up outrageously and went to this hotel to dance and have a good time. I was reminded of it by the lively party of girls.

And I walked back to the Hotel Astor in the brisk evening. I let myself in with the key, because the hotel closed its doors at 6:00 pm. This is what it means to stay at a private hotel.

Monday 21 Aug 2023

They serve breakfast here, in a breakfast room. It is always set up that way, and is only used for breakfast. It is cosy, with built-in seats around the walls. There are paintings on the walls of European forests, or perhaps some of them are English. There are small statues of animals – a wolf, a panther, a dog. We have become accustomed to scorning the sensibilities of the early-to-mid-twentieth century, but I wonder if they deserve reconsideration.

What did they admire? Nature, in all its guises: peaceful, wild, fearful. They seem to accept it all, and don't seem to want to annihilate it. I think we are accustomed to viewing that generation monolithically, as if they all thought the same, but I think they didn't. It was some people who wanted to kill all the thylacines, the Tasmanian tigers, and the eagles, not everyone. The farmers said the thylacines were a threat, and the eagles were too, and other people just thought, for the most part, "Oh well, they must know what they're talking about." And let them do it.

The plates on which I prepared my toast had a picture of Australian scenery and a kookaburra in the middle. We tend to think that the old view of culture was just European, that they saw people as having come to Australia from Europe, and just wanted to make Australia look like Europe: European forests and animals. But then there is the kookaburra on my breakfast plate, as Australian as you could imagine. When we try and sum up the older generations, we oversimplify and fall short.

The tapestry was complex in those days. And they never ordered their meals by clicking on a code and staring at a small rectangle in the palm of their hands. But here we are, saddled with relentless progress. Of course, we are obliged to label it all as progress, uniformly, universally.

Yesterday I saw a completed building. By that I mean I remembered seeing it four years ago, at which time it consisted of a construction space that a building had once occupied, and at the front, a sandstone façade from the old days, propped up with scaffolding. Now the façade has been released from its supports and behind it is a completed building with an outside that is entirely glass. It looks like a see-through building. I applaud it as an attempt to achieve the impossible: to honour the past while making way for a functional present and a viable future.

Addendum

A couple of days later, I walked past again, on the same side of the road as the building, and found a plaque with information about it. It is now a hotel called the Tasman: a luxury hotel. It used to be the head office for a government department: the Public Works Department.

Jobs for the day: I walked down to the Grand Chancellor Hotel to check out procedures for my graduation tomorrow. I wanted to make sure everything will go smoothly tomorrow. I have a choice of cape: either the colour for the Diploma, or I can request the colour for my highest degree, which is the Master of Education from the University of Southern Queensland. As I said to the lady looking after the desk in the Gowns Room, "I don't want to make a big deal out of it, but then again, how many times in my life am I going to do this?"

My job was done in a couple of moments. To get to the Gowns Room I had to walk through dozens of people who were graduating today, and their significant others. They spread around the foyer of the hotel and spilled out into the front courtyard. People were having their photos taken, and smiling. Graduations seem to bring out a lot of smiles. Families were in attendance. Many nationalities were represented, all dressed up brightly and formally – Indian, African, Chinese.

One is never sure these days what to say about the presence of different nationalities. Do critics find this acceptable or permissible? I just want to say I saw many people who represented different cultures, and they were happy to be here. There is something about the awarding of qualifications that makes people happy, especially if they came from another country. They are happy to have completed a course of study, happy to have passed the necessary tests and requirements, happy to be recognised in this society. This is true even if there is no great job on offer, or a terrific new salary. For the moment, the achievement is pleasure enough, and the approval from kin.

I went to the tourist information centre, and that was a good experience. It's nice to talk to someone who is keen to use their knowledge to help you, and that this is built into the culture of the place. I received pertinent advice, I bought tickets, I was acknowledged as a person. This is novel, in the light of going into a restaurant and being pointed towards a piece of paper that displays a QR code. Perhaps one day there will be a revelation that the trade-off for this "greater efficiency" is fundamentally unacceptable.

I assert that "greater efficiency" is very often a myth, and the choice represents, instead, a way of being. When I first started using a computer, around 1986, I tried to put everything on the computer. I spent an inordinate amount of time in organising data and inputting it to the computer. After a while, I realised I had gone too far, and that some things were best left non-digital. In fact, this very decision was the essence of the situation, determining when and when not to use the computer to assist in getting work done.

Of course, people would say that I am talking about situations that no longer apply. I am "out of date". But I am not arguing; I am living in a parallel universe, where things make sense. I live my own peace. I think that the young people I saw interfacing with a QR code were treating the restaurant merely as background, not as a place to be. Perhaps that is true of their whole lives. I am travelling, so I am interested in being in different places, not in watching the same small rectangular device. But I realise there is no way to communicate the message I am trying to articulate when people are enamoured with the devices.

I spent some time walking here and there. Partly that was because I wasn't quite sure where I was going, and partly it was because walking is good for you. It treads out all the stuff in your head that can get sour. That might be when you have spent days and weeks on a task, without taking the time to change the scene. Not a bad thing, but changing the scene, and walking, are healthy.

I found myself in front of the Maritime Museum. I am not a sailor or a boat lover, but I accept that boats and ships have been important in the development of our world, so a museum devoted to that could be interesting. Also, over the last two hundred years (say), boats and ships have been treated aesthetically, so I know they can be elegant. Shapes have been guided by beauty as well as functionality. And I find that things are more interesting when you can see some connection to them, or when they trigger your memory.

The museum was run by volunteers, who probably have a different emotional connection to ships and boats than I do. I think of it in terms of my family history. On both my mother's and my father's side, they lived for hundreds of years in rural areas, not on the coast. They were miners in Cornwall, and trades people in Scotland and Hertfordshire. They did not go to sea, even though the Cornish and the Scots were never far from it.

However, the museum had things that I remembered from when I was young, for example, Tasmania as the Apple Isle. This was true when I was a boy, before the European Common Market put a stop to that very quickly. The government ended up paying farmers to pull out their apple trees. There were many pictures in the museum of the heady days of copious apple exports.

There were also pictures from the convict days, and I have three connections there. And indeed, two of the pictures displayed are ones that I have. One was of the *Waterloo*, which brought out William Archer, my mother's great grandfather, in 1838 as a convict. The picture was of the *Waterloo* in 1842, shipwrecked off the coast of South Africa. It broke up in a storm – the ship was said to be decrepit and half-rotten – with the loss of 143 convicts, fourteen sailors, fifteen soldiers, and eighteen wives and children. But I already thought that William had a lucky life, and he ended up as the publican of his own hotel in Sydney.

The other picture is quite a graceful scene on the docks in London, showing the *St Vincent* ready for departure. I knew this picture because I had seen it before, and I had eventually hunted it down in the British Newspapers database and saved it. It was a hand-drawn picture before the days of photography, drawn by an illustrator in the employ of the *London Illustrated Gazette*. The *St Vincent* was not always used to transport convicts; sometimes it brought free settlers out to Australia. Sarah Crosby, my great great grandmother, came out as a convict on the *St Vincent*, arriving in April 1850, but the drawing was published in 1844.

The *St Vincent* also had the distinction of being the ship that brought the last load of convicts to Van Diemen's Land in 1853, which also happened to be the year that Sarah and Edward got married (in the Church of St Joseph near to the Hotel Astor).

Another exhibit in the museum that jogged my memory was a large model of a ship crashed into a bridge. I remember this happening. It was in January 1975. The tanker, the *SS Illawarra*, had crashed into the Derwent Bridge. The model shows the ship underneath the bridge, resting haplessly against one of the piers. The model was made for the Royal Commission which was set up to investigate the disaster. Included in the model are two tiny cars, models of the ones which ended up perched over the edge at the top, suddenly hovering over the abyss. I remember how shocking and unimaginable it all was at the time.

I didn't expect to see a model of this incident, but I won't say this again, because I don't expect to see most of the things I see in life every day, and certainly not on my trip. Saying it all the time would wear a bit thin.

In the museum there were models and real-life artefacts of grand things and modest things: a dinghy, the cabin of a destroyer, the cabin of a ferry, a light from a lighthouse. The cabin, which was the captain's, showed his bunk and his desk, and his small library of books, with a wooden bar in front of the books so they would not fall out in stormy weather. I guess a captain has some spare time to read, in between captaining and sleeping. I didn't register what the books were.

The last part of the exhibition was an art show in one large gallery room. The pieces had an aquatic theme. The artist was Barbie Kjar. I was looking closely at how the pieces – on textured paper – were attached to the wall. They had no frames, they were just pieces of paper, and they were attached using a drawing pin at each corner. The volunteer who was in the room noticed what I was doing, and asked me if I was an artist. I told him, "No, I am a writer. I write books, but I want to have an exhibition to display my book covers and my explanations of the books."

He thought this was an interesting idea. Then he thought some more, and he made the suggestion that I could approach the museum and see if they were interested in having it there. I said I had to do it first in Sydney, but if it went well, there was the potential to travel it to different places. When we got to the desk at the departure door, he gave me a form which invited people to submit a proposal for an exhibition.

So, that was all encouraging. My idea is not outlandish. Perhaps it is possible, and it will happen.

From one unlikely museum I went to another. There is a museum dedicated to Douglas Mawson, who made the first Australian expedition to Antarctica in 1911. Previously he had been in the team that were the first to reach the South Magnetic Pole in 1908. Other venturers in the Antarctic at this time were Roald Amundsen, a Norwegian, who reached the South Pole in December 1911, and Robert Scott, British, who reached it a month later but died on the return journey. Mawson's expedition was in the name of science.

An expedition in the 1970s visited the camp and made efforts to preserve the buildings. The museum is called a replica museum because it is made up as the living quarters that the team used during their stay in Antarctica.

Antarctic exploration has never been a focus of my interest. However, when I was in the second year of high school, what they now call Year Eight, I won a prize for coming top of my class, and the prize was a book on polar exploration: *Heroes of Polar Exploration*. You could say that that book was one of the early books in what has become my library. The oddity is that Douglas Mawson was not featured in that book, nor even mentioned.

Addendum

I had to check on this when I came home from Tasmania. I remembered the book in Hobart, and I fully expected Mawson to be included in it. It was called *Heroes of Polar Exploration*. It had stories in it about Roald Amundsen and Robert Scott, so, covering the period around 1911, but not a word was there about Douglas Mawson. I was shocked. Why was this? Was it because Mawson established a base and stayed there, whereas Amundsen and Scott were mobile explorers, racing for the South Pole? Mawson's main purpose was said to be science.

This argument does not work. Mawson's expedition explored the surrounding area, and they made many discoveries. I have to examine the genesis of the book. It was published in 1962 by Cassell Caravel, a division of American Heritage Publishing. Was it simply that Mawson was Australian, and Americans ignored (or were ignorant of) Australians? I remain shocked.

I had walked past the Mawson Museum before, and had simply thought, "Why would anyone willingly go to a place where it is freezing all year, and they have no gardens, farms or forests? You can't live there unless you bring everything with you." But, I concede that some humans long to go where no one has been before, and they long to find out about such places. Mawson was a geologist, so he had a perspective of interest.

So, I conceded that humans are endlessly interesting, and I went to the museum. And yes, they did take everything, including tons of coal, and the expedition was funded. The historical perspective is that this was the "Heroic Era of Polar Exploration", in the late 1800s and early 1900s. Just as, nowadays, the interest is in going to the moon and to Mars, and some astronauts are constantly floating above us in the international space station. I concede.

The moment you step into the first corridor of the museum, you hear the sound of the wind. A sign tells you that Antarctica is the windiest place on the planet, and the winds can be hundreds of kilometres per hour in blizzard times. The sound comes through a loudspeaker, howling mercilessly. Many of the explorers did not return. There were numerous trips from the base, and there were mishaps. One man, Ninnis, disappeared down a crevasse with a full dogsled team.

The team was set up to stay for a year. They had a slow-combustion stove, which was fuelled by coal. I could warm to the idea of the stove because I lived in the country for twenty years and I had one, a Scottish-made Wellstood. I burned wood, not coal, and the stove made winters cosy.

The purported purpose of the expedition was science, to investigate this unknown continent. They had instruments and journals. For those interested in real estate, the Mawson expedition's endeavour is largely the basis for Australia's claim to part of Antarctic territory.

I was interested in how a group of men survives for such a long period in a small cabin, besieged by the weather. Authority, discipline, and routines were big contributors to their success, but so too were books. The cabin contained a considerable library, although I should mention that there was also a small musical organ on which they played hymns on Sundays, and there was a record player (1910-style).

I asked the volunteer what she knew about the library. There were many shelves of books around the cabin. The volunteer knew a lot. The library had been well-stocked, and much thought was given to salvaging the books for the museum. One contribution she described was a set of the Encyclopedia Britannica. In 1910, encyclopedias were becoming popular – easy for us to relate to because we now have Google.

There was a new edition out around 1910, and when the publisher found out that the expedition wanted to take a set with them to Antarctica, they donated a set. That set was destroyed during the vicissitudes of the weather over the subsequent fifty years, because it was the 1960s before an expedition went back to the 1911 site. But the next story is that, when the museum was looking for a replacement set, someone found out about it and owned a set of the same edition; they donated it to the museum and that is what is on display.

The volunteer had a great mental knowledge of the range of books in the library. Each person was allowed to bring their own personal collection, and there were books that were brought as a general collection. Some of the books were scientific and technical, but some of them were for entertainment. One story, that came from one of the original team members, was that a small group went on a side expedition, and one person found room for a copy of *Vanity Fair*, a popular novel by Willliam Thackeray, not without its share of romance. After all, one might be pinned down in the same spot, stuck in a tent for the duration of a blizzard, which might last for several days.

By the time I left, I had formed a deeper appreciation of the experiences the men had had, but I had not felt any urge to replicate their experiences. In the shop, I bought a booklet that contained some further information about Hobart and Antarctica: *Hobart's Antarctic History*.

Yes, it's good that we are all different, or wouldn't it be a boring world? You know, that speech. But there is something more, for the people who led the expedition, and those who accompanied the leaders, didn't just say they wanted to do this, they put forward justifications for it. It was for king (as it was then), and country (or empire), and the cause of science.

When I am doing something, let's say, writing a book about pieces of my past, do I say I am doing it for king (as it is now), and country, or science or literature? It's just a private passion, or interest, or whim. The wind is howling in my ears, and I am driven on. There is no flagpole outside my library. My interests are not patriotic. What then?

Lunch, a meal. Humans are easily distracted by hunger, thirst, or a full bladder.

I had purchased a ticket for an afternoon harbour cruise, although the Derwent River doesn't have that enclosed feeling you get in Sydney Harbour. It's too open and river-like. The boat completed a large circle over an hour or two, coming back to the spot from which it had left. It was logical, but it seemed artificial. Nevertheless, it was enjoyable, and I am enlarging my concept of Hobart. I might say, I feel I am getting to know it better.

The captain kept up a non-stop flow of commentary, from the historical to the contemporary. There was the threat of the Russians in Tasmania, and the threat of Wrest Point Casino to the social fabric of the town. When I boarded the boat, the captain asked me where I was from. When I said "Sydney", he told me that he had come from Sydney, too, although his version of Sydney was Palm Beach, not the western suburbs where I grew up, or the northwest of Sydney where I live now. Palm Beach is its own little world. But I was impressed that the captain had learned the commentary convincingly, and had integrated it into his personal outlook. He said that Hobart was a good place to live.

I went back to the hotel, and I had a yoga session booked for the evening on Zoom. The next day I noticed that there is a yoga studio just around the corner from the hotel, although I am not doing anything with this knowledge. I didn't have dinner, and it didn't seem to matter. I had thought that sushi would be a good choice, because I could buy it before the yoga session, and it wouldn't matter that it was cold two hours later.

It was a good yoga session, despite the less-than-Ideal conditions. The Zoom connection worked satisfactorily.

Tuesday 22 Aug 2023

Today is the day of my graduation from the Diploma of Family History course at the University of Tasmania. At 10:00 am at the Grand Chancellor Hotel. I had checked in the day before to see that all would go smoothly. I had breakfast in the Hotel Astor's breakfast room, dressed myself suitably and walked down the hill to the venue, all in good time. I did not wear a suit and tie. I don't usually wear a tie these days, although I still have a cupboard full of them. (However, a friend has since reminded me that I recently bought a tie from a Scottish shop, in the Mackie family tartan – my mother's side of the family. If I had remembered that, I might have worn it. Life always manages to be imperfect, even in inconsequential ways.)

I didn't bring an umbrella, even though the sky looked threatening. I arrived to find a great mass of people, swarming. Several students arrived already dressed in their gowns, one girl with silver shoes – very nice, wouldn't you say? The overwhelming impression was: families. More than anything, today was a celebration of families, all the different configurations: mothers and fathers proud of daughters graduating, of sons graduating, and sons and daughters proud of mothers graduating, or fathers. I am convinced I saw it all. And often, it was just a mother or a father, not both, because that's the way it so often is these days.

I found my way to the room where I would pick up my gown and cape and headdress. Then I found my way to the space where university folk would fit you out properly, fussing over you until the hat was on straight, the cape fell off your shoulders with just the right fold, and the gown was neat and in order. I realised it was twenty years since I last graduated – 2003, when I received my Master of Education degree from the University of Southern Queensland (at a ceremony held at a hotel in Sydney). I was happy to let the staff fuss over me for a moment. It is not the sort of attire that I am accustomed to wearing regularly.

While we were waiting outside the hall, I decided I needed a photo of myself in my regalia, so I asked two women who were waiting near me. One was the mother and the other was the partner of a man receiving a degree in music. They were happy to oblige, so at least I had a photo to send today to friends and family. I found my seat: in the middle in the third row, so, a "ringside" seat.

The ceremony went smoothly. Universities could be described as high users of ceremony, as much as churches and law courts. Accordingly, they have the procedures and the skills in place. Our ceremony included a four-person musical ensemble consisting entirely of brass instruments: two trumpets, a trombone, and a French horn. They played the national anthem, and a processional to accompany the academics making their way to their seats so they could sit there silently and patiently for the next hour and a half.

There were speeches and congratulations aplenty. And it's true: the ceremony marked a completion for every student here, and many who were not there – students from my course came from all around Australia, so not everyone was in attendance. Online learning has its benefits. And a few students here were about to receive their PhD: Doctorate of Philosophy, for their special knowledge acquired in a narrow field.

I didn't continue with my PhD back in 2011 (a proposed thesis on ethics), parting ways with the university after twelve months. After a while, I came to the conclusion that this was a good thing. I didn't need to do it, and there was nothing to be gained by doing it. It was better for me to concentrate on writing my own books and to continue with that. But all praise to the people standing here today.

I went through the motions, joining the queue standing at the side of the hall and listening to the names being called out, coming up onto the stage at the right time, tipping my headdress when my name was called, standing on the spot marked "X" to have my photo taken, then moving off to the side of the stage where I was handed my diploma, then down the steps to return to my seat.

That process was repeated about two hundred times, and all the while the Chancellor, Alison Watkins, stood mid-stage and smiled. My one disappointment was that she just stood there. My one desire in this whole cheerful charade was to have my photo taken with the Chancellor shaking my hand, and us holding my certificate together. That certainly used to be the case, when I received my Bachelor of Business and my Master of Education. I blame COVID: too much risk of transferral of germs. But now there is no soul.

The brass ensemble played another tune while the academics moved off. To my great amusement, the tune was that of my high school anthem: Strathfield South High School ("Strathfield South keep fine and free, honour and integrity...." "Integrity" was the school's motto). It had been a new school just prior to my going there, and one of the music teachers had chosen the tune and written the lyrics. Today, I am sure I could look up Google and find the words, but I will refrain from that.

When all the words had been spoken, we students were asked to stand and turn around and applaud all the people in the audience: partners, family and friends, who had supported us through our studies and who had come today to witness our achievement. I clapped my hands along with the other students, to applaud the audience for what they had done for their family and friends, and for those back home who cared about me.

After the pomp and ceremony, there was a morning tea in a huge auditorium, which may explain why the ceremony was held at the hotel rather than the university. I was standing there watching the flow of people and the chatter, when the lady who had taken my photo for me walked up and said she had seen me walking onto the stage, and she took a video of the scene. She would send it to my email. I was surprised and delighted, and I gave her my business card.

It is perhaps anachronistic for me to call it my business card when I am, to all intents and purposes, retired. Nevertheless, it still accurately describes what I do, writing in various fields of interest.

While I was still standing there, I saw the Chancellor nearby, so I went over to talk. She seemed like a nice person, and in any case, it was an admirable feat to smile for over an hour non-stop at a procession of around two hundred students, to acknowledge each one on their achievement. And without any actions to enliven the moments, like a handshake. I said hello, and she replied, "Let me think. Your name was.... Martin?"

I was impressed, and said so. I told her my name. She said she had been a teacher, and you inevitably try to remember everyone's name. I had to smile, and said I remembered that from my days as a schoolteacher. What I came to say was that I was here graduating, but if any of my lecturers were here, I would not recognise them, and I explained that my course was in online mode. I hastened to say that I appreciated the opportunity that the online mode gave me, particularly during the time of COVID.

She consulted with a colleague, and then told me that the coordinator of the course would have been here today, but she was ill. She said that her colleague would see if any other of my lecturers were around. Then I drifted off to the massive hall.

There were foodstuffs abounding, and drinks. Wines and beers were available, and party pies, and dips and sushi. I know some people wade in when free food is on the table, but my appetite wanes at such times. I think I am alert to other people and ready to engage in interaction. I don't want to be engrossed in food. I had some sushi and a green tea. I sound like a monk.

I walked around the huge space. People were flocking. There was a band along one wall, playing nice music that no one will ever remember. There was a gift shop at one end. For example, you could buy a sweater with the university logo. And there was an entire table with stuffed bears. I could have bought a soft toy to commemorate my studies. I did not.

In one corner there was a photography setup, with a large screen with a Tasmanian forest image as the backdrop. But there was a difference: the person being photographed stood on a small platform, and there was a halo of light on a long pole that rotated around the platform. There was a camera attached to the inside of the halo. What happened? The halo moved fast around in a circle, and it took a video. The person could move – smile, wave, or dance. And they would send it to your email. Free, courtesy of the university.

I did it, but it will be awful. The best I could do was smile. I suppose that is something, but what does it mean? If anyone watched it, what would they make of it? Would they be amazed, dazzled? I wonder why I have to be a part of this society. So much technology, so little sense. And then I sound like a stick in the mud.

When I had had enough of the morning tea, I left. I took my gown back to the Gown Room. The lady in front of me in the queue said she was receiving her degree after four years. She finished just as COVID started and lockdowns commenced. She had come over from Melbourne for the ceremony. We get to keep the little black flat-top cap with the pompom down the side.

I walked out of the hotel, carrying my diploma in an envelope under my arm, and it was drizzling. In fact, you would call it a heavy drizzle. It was about fifteen minutes' walk to the hotel, and I thought I had better not get the diploma wet. That would be a sad end. So, I flagged down a taxi. This turned out to be an experience.

I remembered the address of the hotel and I told that to the taxi driver. He tapped that into his navigator. I thought that was ominous. The Hotel Astor is one hundred years old. Normally you would expect a taxi-driver to know where it was. I guessed that the taxi driver was a recent immigrant. Now here is the funny bit. He drove around the corner, less than two blocks, and pulled over. I thought, "Why is he pulling over? We've only just begun." But he told me that we had reached the destination. It was not the destination; it was the side wall of a three-storey brick building. It wasn't even in the right street.

He gestured to the navigator, and told me that according to the navigator, we had arrived. I said we had not arrived, and I said I would tell him the way to go. Me, the visitor from Sydney! So, I accurately guided him up the hill, through turns at three corners, because there were one-way streets in this vicinity.

When we arrived, I pointed to the name of the hotel. I think he still didn't get it, and I couldn't figure out what it was he wasn't getting. But I got there, and I was relatively dry which, after all, was the point of the venture.

If I talk to friends and family about what I did for the rest of the day, they would probably be disappointed. Why wasn't I out having lunch with newfound friends, drinking champagne and laughing? But I did have a laugh, about the strangeness of the taxi driver experience. I noted that the rain cleared up after this.

I went down the road from the hotel and found a Thai café where I had lunch, a very satisfying curry amid a steady flow of lunch-time diners.

I went to the State Library and asked them if they could tell me where the Police Magistrates Office was located in 1852. That summoned up a flurry of maps, ones that could be superimposed on each other, so you could compare nowadays with the historical period. It was all good fun. In the end it was inconclusive. However, the lady did find a picture of two buildings in a street, looking down towards the water, and it's very possible that one of them is the Police Magistrates Office.

The importance is that Edward Lewis and Sarah Crosby had to meet if they were to get married, so where was he and where was she? She was assigned to work in the Police Magistrates Office (PMO on her convict record card). I assume her job was cleaning (or, more generally, domestic servant), because she didn't read or write. And Edward, by now a young policeman, was assigned to the Police Barracks. This used to be on the corner of one street, but then it was moved, so it all gets tricky.

Well, enough for now. I went walking again. I walked past the Gaol, which also housed a church and it was called the Penitentiary. Punishment and reform were so haplessly intertwined. Down the road from there I looked at the Scots Church, or St Andrew's, now a Uniting Church. Its history was told in plaques outside in the lawns. It included the fact that one minister was terminated because he tried to kiss the wife of one of the church's wardens. Sad to have that perpetuated on a plaque unto the ends of time.

I found the current magistrates court, because I thought it may have some information about its history, like the plaques in the churchyard. But I came face to face with Security, that's all, and the man couldn't reconcile what I said with his job description. "You would have to talk to someone else." So, to no avail.

Dinner at a Nepalese restaurant: very acceptable.

For the record, my room number at the hotel was "4"; it was on the first floor, down the hall from the breakfast room with its various paintings, statues of animals and a beautiful Chinese vase. There was no chair in my room, but the room was roomy enough for me to do yoga, and the furniture was lovely.

Wednesday 23 Aug 2023

I departed on Wednesday morning. I have booked into the Shipwrights Arms Hotel at Battery Point. This suburb is a mystery to me. I had not paid attention to it on my visits to Tasmania before, despite the fact that this is my fourth visit. I decided to walk to it. It was not raining, and there were no hills for me to have to climb. I carried my backpack and wielded my suitcase on its trusty wheels. The wheels made a lot of noise, to my ears, anyway. That was the only downside.

It took me twenty minutes of steady walking, and I found the hotel easily enough. I asked one gentleman where Trumpeter Street was, and he obliged. The hotel was opened in 1846, with some renovations since then, but it has been operating continuously. It was built to provide accommodation for locals who worked in ship-building. You look down the street and you can see the water: the Derwent River. You can see the other side of the river, which is, I suppose, one or two kilometres away. There is something magical about that.

I arrived there mid-morning with the intention of leaving my suitcase and going for a walk around Battery Point. The door was not locked, and I went in. There was a door to a bar on my left and a corridor ahead to a bar and restaurant, which had plentiful light. But here, in the entry area, it was as dark as a cave. A young man called out to me cheerily to see what I wanted at this hour of the morning, and he was in darkness, just a silhouette. Why? There seemed to be no reason.

Life is amusing. He led me up to a reception desk, behind which, not one, not two, but three young women sat, obviously waiting for my entrance. I told the young man the nature of my visit, and he spent time looking at the computer, presumably to verify my booking. He did so, and agreed that they would look after my suitcase for the rest of the morning, and I could return about twelve-thirty. I thought this was an agreeable arrangement. One of the three ladies rose to approach my resting suitcase to put it in a more suitable position.

I walked down many of the streets, which I found enchanting. I wonder what it is. Is it the particular age of things: a hundred to almost two hundred years old? Is it the fact that you can tell that most of the houses were built by people who were well-off? And even the workmen's cottages could only be purchased today by those who are well-off? Or is it the easy co-existence of the fancy houses and the workmen's cottages?

One of the things that resonated most was the houses and yards that looked like country towns did sixty years ago, when I was a child. It could be a sprawling tree or vine, an unusual pine tree or a magnolia in full bloom, or vines running over a fence as if to swallow it. Or a backyard with a car sitting there, that had been dormant for a decade or more.

Or was it the suburb itself, the slow flow of people, an old, shuffling man, an old woman unsteady on her feet, alongside the young florist bringing a new display out to the front of her shop, that was housed in a stone cottage from the 1880s? And the presence of people walking their dogs, an entirely modern phenomenon, looking alert and breezy.

Whatever it was, there was something dreamy about it, as if this was a place where you didn't have to have an excuse for having done nothing all morning. And the silence. The streets were silent. It's funny when you think whether people make a lot of noise in the city. In fact, they don't, but there is still the altogether-hum, and the interruptions are more frequent. And there is the speed of it. When a person comes into view, they are moving at a pace, because they are going somewhere, and of course it must be of some importance or urgency; it must have to be done soon.

The busiest place in Battery Point was one café, which was at the intersection of two roads and which had three huge windows, so that the people in the café were like an exhibition: "Jackman & McRoss, Bakers of Fine Breads, Cakes & Pastries". I thought it might be a pleasant interlude, and I enjoyed a mixed fruit tart with coffee.

I walked back to the hotel, checked in and found my room. It was on the first floor looking down on the quiet street. If you leant right to the edge of the window, you could just see the water between the houses. The furniture in this room is not interesting, and indeed, there is not much of it, but there is a chair and table in one corner. Across the corridor there is a small kitchenette. One must be grateful for what is offered.

I am staying here for four nights. Tomorrow night is a jazz night at the hotel: perfect!

I found a different way to walk back to Salamanca. It's only a ten-minute walk. I am mentally mapping it, although that does not include all the street names. I was indecisive about lunch, because I had had a late morning tea, but in the end I decided to do it. Then I was indecisive about what I wanted, but in the end I decided on sushi.

I went into a café near the wharves. There were choices in the window, and I decided on what I wanted. I told the Japanese lady, and she motioned me to a table in the windowed corner, with a nice view of the wharves, the boats and the water. As I sat down, she then motioned to the machine on the table: "If you want to order a drink or anything else, please use the machine."

I groaned. I am being pursued. I will be run out of town. I turned to face her. I said, "I do not wish to use the device. May I please order tea from you?"

She was instantly gracious and said, "Of course, sir", and soon brought me tea. I enjoyed my meal. When I went to pay, I said to her, "I do not wish to be critical, and I really enjoyed my lunch. But I am not ready to use the machine to order my meals. Perhaps I will be one day, but not at the moment."

Her response was to laugh outrageously, and she thanked me and wished me well. So that was an experience.

Next, I decided that I wanted to get out of Hobart one day and see some forest. I know there are big trees south of Hobart. It was a question of whether I could get there without a car. I am resolved not to hire a car on this trip. I went to the Tourist

Information Centre, because they can answer questions like that more quickly than I can find out.

Side note

Most writers today, including, sadly, journalists, would have said "quicker" in the previous sentence. I give up, I think the cause is already lost. When you are describing a noun, you use an adjective (quicker); when you are describing a verb, you use an adverb (more quickly). Where were all the teachers a few years ago? They have failed the next generation. What is the noun I was referring to? What is the verb I was referring to? They are the questions a writer must ask. Where were the teachers? It's sad, because if you use the language wrongly, it's still wrong, and it grates. It's hard enough to convey meaning without getting the grammar of expressions wrong.

I also think that this error is sometimes committed consciously, as if the writer thinks that the rule is a bad or unnecessary one, and that with persistent use (or as I would say, repetition of the error), within a generation the rule will have been forgotten. I do not deny that this may be true, but I still regard it as an act of laziness or shoddiness that demonstrates a lack of understanding of, or respect for, the language.

The tourist place did indeed have answers, and now I am booked on a tour for Friday. They will even pick me up from my hotel at 8:00 am. I will see big trees.

I walked past the Mawson's Hut Replica Museum again, and I got a photo of the outside, because I hadn't done that the other day. The photos are like additions to my notes. Just past it, I noticed there was a small shop that sold prints of antique maps. Well, I had seen it before, but I didn't think it was relevant. But where had I been yesterday? The State Library, to find a street map of Hobart around 1852. The shop was certainly relevant: I wanted an antique map.

I went in. There was no one there. The door at the back was open. There were prints displayed around the room, not maps, but old pictures of people and animals and plants. Taking my time, I did see a few maps, such as a world map from the 1600s that showed the coast of Australia, but with the east coast missing. Part of the Tasmanian coast was shown, and some of New Zealand. This reflected the voyage of the Dutchman Abel Tasman, whose statue I had just seen in a park nearby.

Soon, a man made his appearance: old, sparse of hair, and neatly bearded. He was surprised to find a person had come into his shop, but he had the familiarity of space, as if he had been there for many decades. His name was Gerard Willems. I said I had a rather specific question: did he have a map of Hobart streets in 1852 or thereabouts? He pondered. I could tell he was pondering over a wide field. From under the desk he hauled out a book that was, to use ordinary language, falling apart. It would have been over a hundred years old, in my loosely informed assessment.

He flicked through it until he found a street map of Hobart about halfway through. The date on it was 1854. Just about perfect. Then he told me about the map, which he said he may or may not have. About thirty years ago, he made a copy of the map, the original of which is around A3-size. The person he made it for wanted it jazzed up a bit, so he put some colour in the print. The recipient was a collector of sorts. A few years ago, an acquaintance told him he had bought this map at a Melbourne auction for $1,500.

Gerard, the shop-man, asked to see it, and he told the man, "That's not the original. It's the copy I made years ago. You've been duped." Gerard also spoke to the dealer, and the dealer gave the man his money back. That's one story.

I told Gerard I was doing family history, and that's why I wanted to see the map. He said he could make a copy of it, and he would charge me about $20. I was happy with that. He said to come back in a couple of days and he would let me know. While this conversation was going on, a pile of frames stacked against a chair kept falling over, and he kept pushing them back upright.

I had another question. I had been to Tasmania a few years ago and went to a town on the east coast – Swansea, and they were having an exhibition of hand-painted native plants and flowers painted by a local woman in around the 1850s. She knew about print-making and had prepared prints for a book that was eventually published in London. I wondered if some of the prints I was looking at in the shop were hers.

He said, "Yes," and told me her name was Louisa Anne Meredith. Ah, yes, that was it! So, these prints were from her! He had about six on display, and said they were on high-quality paper and used high-quality inks. He could frame them as well if I wanted that. Then, he reached into the piles of papers below his desk and pulled out two books of Meredith's paintings. They were the ones printed in the 1850s (*My Home in Tasmania*, 1852, and *Some of My Bush Friends in Tasmania*, 1860). I had read about these books when I went to the exhibition. He said you might pay thousands of dollars for things like this. With maps, you might pay tens of thousands of dollars.

It was all quite a feast. Then you start to wonder what conversation there is between people in the commercial sphere, who sometimes deal with very rich clients who like to collect things of perceived value, and people in public and academic spheres. And then I wander into a dusty, apparently disorganised shop with metaphorical dust in the air, wondering how he survives from week to week. Who is the naïve one?

This afternoon I needed my umbrella for a period just exceeding five minutes. Then the sun reappeared: no, it didn't, yes, it did. It was like that all afternoon. They have fast weather in Hobart.

I came back to the Shipwrights Arms Hotel for dinner, because it seemed the appropriate thing to do, the first night of my stay. I chose something with a seafood flavour: chowder. I haven't had chowder since I went to England in 2018. It was a big thick soup with various types of fish, including prawns. Very tasty. The company was a noisy riffraff of men, mostly working in the construction industry from what I could make out of their conversation. Friendly banter.

I finished reading an e-book: *A Psalm for the Wild-Built*, by Becky Chambers. Science fiction, I suppose. I understand the title now that I've read the book, but it would take me some time to explain the title, so I won't. It was a prosaic story – this happened and then that happened – about a person who was a "tea monk", a version of "coffee and counselling". It ended up as a conversation between the monk and a robot about whether we need purpose in life to have a worthwhile life. Fair enough, worth thinking about.

Thursday 24 Aug 2023

I had a decent night. Since coming to Tasmania, mostly I have been sleeping through the night. It could be because there is more action and activity in my days, more new things, than when I am at home, so I am more tired. This hotel is better and worse than the Hotel Astor. The latter's walls are thicker; here it seems like the walls are thin. Perhaps it is because the corridor is narrow; if I poke my elbows out, I can touch both walls.

The same business occurs with the shower: you're not sure which tap is hot and cold, so you run both for more than a minute, et cetera. But eventually the hot water comes and you get on with having a shower.

There is no breakfast room here. Well, there is a kitchenette, and it has portions of jams and vegemite, and there is a toaster (and a kettle), but there is no bread. There is a toaster but there is no bread; and there is no shop nearby, and I am not interested in buying a loaf of bread. Amusing. It is a minor thing; I usually only eat fruit salad and yoghurt for breakfast. I am on tour. I adapt.

I have no plans today. I have allowed this situation to develop deliberately. Rarely do I have nothing to do, so the question arises, what does one do when one has no plans? Is it a potentially fearful situation, is it shameful, or is it simply wasteful? Or does inspiration or serendipity occur?

One answer to this quandary is that if one allows things simply to occur, one generally falls into an habitual path, which usually follows our more fearful nature, not our best lights. So, there is a subtlety here, of being alert to good possibilities rather than negativism. And there is also chance at play. It is not a simple thing to be at the mercy of the moment.

Do I have a loose plan, or are there options? Do I have a loose idea of what Hobart is and what I haven't seen of it that I would like to see? Hobart is not a big city, and it is walled in between the river and Mount Wellington (Kunanyi), so I have seen the bulk of it. Are there things that I would like to see again, remembering that often, the same things turn out not to be the same after all (but sometimes they do)?

For example, I went to the State Library the other day, where I had been before, but I had different questions to ask. It was quite a different experience. One is always trying to avoid the trivial and the boring. Some people, in order to achieve this, go in search of danger, like water-skiing or parachuting. Afterwards, they say they felt really alive. My question is, how do feel now? Are you relying on that past experience to justify your life now?

I'm not serious about that question. Everybody is on their own path. However, I am not interested in being seduced into performing dangerous stunts in order to prove to myself or others that I am alive. I could defy people to sit in silence and allow the world to come into view. But I am not asking. What am I saying? I could be saying: don't doubt me. You will not push me where I know I don't want to go, but don't feel sorrow for me because I "haven't lived yet". I am living.

I have been living all this time. I have been living like the moss on a rock. I am in communion with the rock and the weather. The only threat to me is the human who comes and wants to kick me off the rock because they have the blind mentality and unharnessed energy of a vandal. Left to live, I may live forever, evolving into life forms that an artist might come and paint, and then I would be a picture in a gallery, and people would come to see the art and say, "Isn't that beautiful?"

Then there would be a man in a print shop who has been there for years, and around his shop are all sorts of prints that people come in to buy, and they will treasure them. They will hang them in their study and tell their visitors about the funny little shop where they bought it.

After I had completed my morning ablutions and done my homework (checking email and writing my notes), I went to the kitchenette to rinse out my cup. To my surprise, there were two fresh loaves of bread there! Moreover, one was wholemeal and one was sourdough. If I had ordered two loaves of bread, that is what I would have ordered.

To show my gratitude, I made toast and had another cup of tea. Then I had to decide where to eat it, because I did not want to eat it in my bedroom. However, at the end of our corridor there was a small loungeroom, small but full of light because it had bow windows, five of them in an arc. It was a most enjoyable way to have a light breakfast, looking out on the street below, and out at the water.

Still, I had no plan for the day. This was getting serious. But one can always walk, so I left the hotel and walked towards Salamanca market. There are so many interesting houses; I found lots that I hadn't even noticed the other day. I walked down through the shopping centre towards the bottom end of town, where the road heads north to Launceston.

There was a sign for a second-hand bookshop called "Cracked and Spineless", a bold effort at distinctiveness. I am sure I had been there before, but a bookshop is never the same twice. It was small and crowded, as is the way. It is more of an effort these days, as my interests have broadened. There were small alcoves, maybe ten or more of them. I did what I could, not wanting to find anything, because then I would have to carry it!

Nevertheless, I found something. A surprise: *Ultima Thule*, by Henry Handel Richardson. The background is that when I went to Victoria a while ago to spend Christmas with family, I paid a visit to Chiltern. My great great grandfather, Thomas Martin, had lived there in his last days (he died in 1904), and I wanted to see his grave.

While in town, I went into a second-hand shop (not a book shop). The lady was telling me about Richardson, a female author (first name Edith) of the early twentieth century, and the trilogy she had written: *The Fortunes of Richard Mahony*. She actually had the first two books of the trilogy in the shop, in paperback. The first volume was *The Way Home*; the second was *Australia Felix*. She did not have the third volume, *Ultima Thule*.

I bought the two books, of course, and that commenced a hunt for the third. In a second-hand bookshop in Sydney, I found a hardback of the trilogy, which was satisfying, but I still wanted the paperback of the third book. And here it was, in Hobart.

I took the book to the counter, and told the two men (one old, one young) the story. I told them I was breaking a rule by buying books, given my situation as a traveller. But the young man had something more to offer. He asked me whether I had all of her books. He didn't seem to be interested in my rule. He said, "I'll bet we've got one book of hers that you haven't got", and he walked over to a different section of the shop and grabbed the book straight away. His knowledge was unerring.

What was the book? *Myself when Young*. He explained that it was an autobiography of her childhood which she wrote late in life. I hadn't heard of it. She didn't get to finish the book; a friend of hers took over and finished it. This is all explained in the book, a slim paperback. I was delighted, so I ended up buying two books, instead of one, or instead of none!

Perhaps I have some sympathy with Richardson because, until the publication of *Ultima Thule*, her work was not popular, and she considered herself to be a failure. Her earlier work had been described as "dull but honest", and one critic had opined that *Australia Felix* might have been written by a retired grocer. *The Way Home* was thought to lack story, and atmosphere.

Nevertheless, a century later, her books had become well-enough known to still be in print and floating around second-hand bookshops like Jane Austen novels. And miraculously, I had found the third book in her trilogy, along with the bonus of a book of hers that I had not heard of. This happened on my day with no plan.

I went from there toward the wharves; one is always going towards the wharves in Hobart. Suddenly I realised I was in the same spot where the taxi-driver had stopped the other day to try to let me off, telling me we had arrived. I had a thought. The address of the Hotel Astor is 157 Macquarie Street. I wondered what the address of this place was.

I walked around the corner, into Macquarie Street. The building was the Hobart Town Hall. I thought, a building of such a nature has to have a number on it. The Council would have been proud to do so.

And sure enough, the number of the building was 57. The taxi-driver had misheard me, and typed 57 into the navigator instead of 157. It all made sense. Unfortunately, I don't think it had made sense to him. Amusing.

I was at the end of town where Henry Jones built up a hugely successful business making jams from fresh fruit. This was in the era when Tasmania was the Apple Isle. The buildings have been taken over by other purposes. The University of Tasmania has one part for an arts centre.

I went into a small exhibition. Maybe it was a student project. It was limited in scope. The theme was "Reaching for the Stars". There was a video which had music and an idea, the idea that it is inherently human to identify with the stars, and to want to reach for them, and if we fall, the worst we do is fall back to earth. Along the wall there was a fragile hanging made out of string or wire, with the shapes of stars hanging on vertical lines. In the middle of the floor there were two crumpled stars, made out of material that looked like that used for flagons of wine, I guessed.

What did I think? It was interesting. I guess the first thing I look for is coherence, and it achieved that. Was it profound? It was a simple assertion, but it was a positive sentiment, and I prefer that to nihilism.

From there I went into an adjacent space, and this was high-end, commercial space. Items were for sale, like hall tables out of Huon Pine for around $1,500. There were items in steel, glass, ceramics and wool; all creative, all beautiful. It must be a different life to have disposable wealth where one can decide to purchase such an item and, of course, have it delivered to one's home wherever one lives. But still, very nice to look at.

You could walk through into a courtyard which had an open-air café and was part of the Henry Jones Art Hotel. Beyond the courtyard was another gallery, showing an exhibition that was on for six weeks. The artist was a woman who had moved from Europe to Australia, and she had made pictures reflecting her transition. Kate Piekutowski: "Between Two Cities". The pictures were etchings.

I found them all relatable: a woman, a bicycle, a suitcase, city buildings as the surroundings, a vase of sunflowers. They all had the aura of self-awareness, accepting of life as it happens, whether or not one has a plan.

I needed lunch, something light. I found a café I had looked at previously but not entered. Places have to have the right vibe, with people happy to go there and be there, but they should still preserve an air of quietness. I had a toasted cheese sandwich and a pot of Earl Grey tea. It came in a cast iron pot. Perfect.

There was still much of the day in front of me, and I was not going to repeat things I had already done. But I needed to walk. Walking walks off many thoughts that can become fetid. I decided I would walk up towards Cascades Female Factory. I had been there twice before, but I might not even get there, and if I did, it was about the right distance.

I walked up a different street from my previous visit, as it ascended a hill. I walked past Barrack Street, which was the street where the Military Barracks had been located. The military barracks had included a military prison, and the site is still occupied by the Army. But Edward Lewis had been in the police force, not the military.

I walked on. I went past the intersection where you turn left to go to the university. That's good to know, but I don't need to go there. I had just had the thought that I had finished a diploma through the university, but geographically, I couldn't find my way there.

I continued towards Cascades. At a certain point, I turned off the road and headed down to a creek; fresh water bubbled its way along. The first time I had been to Cascades, I had taken a wrong turn early on, and found myself climbing high above the main road, on the suburban backroads. Eventually I had found a track coming back down, and it had meandered along the creek and eventually arrived at the Female Factory.

This time, I found myself in the carpark of a church: C3 Church, which I recognised from Sydney, although I didn't know it existed outside of Sydney. From where it was, I had the thought that in the four years since I had been here, the Female Factory had been bulldozed away, and replaced by the C3 Church. You know, those catastrophic thoughts that spring into your mind when faced with something quite unexpected?

It was ridiculous, of course. The Female Factory was a World Heritage site.

I kept walking, and then my progress was stopped by a small group of people whose attention was focused on a certain part of the creek. That was extremely unusual. Some had cameras or phones trained on the creek. One had a very expensive camera with a telephoto lens. When I got close, I realised they were being very quiet too. I went up close to one lady and whispered, "What's going on?" She whispered, "There is a platypus in the water."

I didn't see the platypus, but I didn't really expect to. They are shy. I lived next to a creek in northern New South Wales for twenty years, and I saw a platypus only once – actually, there were two. It was during a flood, and I was standing on the wooden bridge near my house, and they were swimming against the torrent. Clearly, they are strong. Frankly, I thought that the only reason I saw them even then was because they couldn't hear me. The noise of the flood was too loud.

I was happy that other people had seen it. Later in the day, I was talking to a friend on the phone, and I told him this story. He told me that this platypus, or this spot in the creek, had been on a television program, because a man who had a terminal illness had discovered the platypus and taken an interest in it. The experience had been restorative for him. Maybe that's why numerous people had come to this spot today.

In a few minutes, I arrived at Cascades Female Factory. It was completely different. The last time I had been here, it had consisted of the rebuilt sandstone walls, the matron's house, and a small office: that's all. There had been an installation in one of the yards consisting of a tapestry made up of metal squares, about two metres by two metres. I had taken a picture of it, and used it on the cover of one of my books: *The Quilt Approach*.

This time, there was an impressive new building, which must have cost more than a million dollars. It housed a museum area as well as the reception and shop. The metal installation of the patchwork quilt was gone.

I enjoyed my visit. All of the spaces I visited had been refreshed, and more information was available. In the bottom yard, which was where the mothers and their babies were housed, there was an enormous aluminium etching, perhaps five metres long and one and a half metres high. It had inscribed on it, in handwriting, the names of all the babies that were recorded during the time of the prison: their births and deaths. There were thousands.

On this huge panel, I found Mary Ann Crosby, Sarah's baby that was born in April 1851. It was a good thing I knew the date of birth, because the names were in chronological order, not alphabetical order. It showed her birth date, but not her death.

The lady at reception was very interested in my story and was very helpful. She thought that, because Mary Ann Crosby's date of death was not shown, it probably meant she had been sent to the Female Orphan School, the records of which are managed by a separate organisation. She gave me the details for contacting them.

I looked through the Matron's Cottage, which was the only building left standing after the twentieth century. Nobody had wanted any sign of the Female Factory to be left. It was a good job that I had visited before, because most of the items that had been on display then were gone. The interesting aspect now was the reference to a place called the Messengers' Room.

The Factory employed two policemen who conveyed messages to and from police headquarters in Hobart. They were always on call. The room where they stayed was shut off from the rest of the Matron's Cottage, with its own separate entrance, because the policemen were not to have any interaction with the inmates.

The question that came to my mind was whether Edward Lewis had ever been one of these messengers, because he could have met Sarah that way, when she was here. The actuality of life in those days was seldom as strict or compliant as the authorities wanted it to be.

The lady at reception told me I might find out in the database, because the messengers were employees of the Female Factory, and the database listed employees. There is always hope, and there is always work left to do.

When my head was full at the Female Factory, I left and walked up to the township. It was time for a coffee. There was a wholefoods store which looked very pleasant, and it seemed that they had a couple of stools for people to sit on, so I went in and ordered a coffee. I sat down at the stool. There were a few books on the table for people to view while they were sipping coffee. A couple of them were children's books, which I suspect were written by people who were part of the whole-foods throng. They were nicely done.

I looked at the other books. A friend of mine had found out recently that she has osteoporosis, and this was a surprise to her. She is investigating the views of various practitioners, and saw an acupuncturist, who told her that bone broth is very helpful. She thought this was an unusual recommendation, and so did I. Now, the title of the book I was looking at was *Bone Broths*. I have never in my life seen a book of that title. Naturally, I had to buy the book. It was a day of serendipity.

I walked back to the hotel, the Shipwrights Arms. Tonight was the jazz night at the hotel. The band played in the bar, a small bar that could only hold thirty or forty people at its fullest. In the bar, you can see why this place is renown for being the end point of the Sydney-Hobart Yacht Race. The walls are plastered with framed

42

photos of yacht races, going back decades. It is down the road at Battery Point that the yachts berth.

The band consisted of four players: a drummer, who must have been in his eighties, a bass player in his late seventies singing some of the songs and playing the most magnificent old wooden double bass, a guitar player who may have been in his thirties and who was very accomplished, and a lady singer who had a silken voice. They say it was jazz, but there are myriad forms of music that are called jazz. The instruments set the scene: the guitar was a lovely wooden piece that looked about thirty years old and very cool and professional. The man was relaxed and fluid in his playing. He had well-groomed black hair, an evocation of Johnny Cash.

The songs ranged from jazz classics (I only remember the song title "Mack the Knife", but there were many others), to old rock: Johnny Cash songs, Van Morrison, and even The Rolling Stones. The audience was not the raging teens and twenties; they were two or three generations beyond that. A few of them got up to dance as the night wore on. I heard one man say afterwards, "The thing about dancing is that it makes you forget where you put your beer".

A lady spoke to me, and wanted to talk. She was on holidays with a couple of other ladies from rural Victoria, and she wanted to meet people. They were around sixty. She told me the abbreviated story of her life, and wanted my story, in a few words. Yes, I have versions of that, and I gave her one of those: failed relationships and compensatory children. She invited me to join the two friends who were with her. She had had more to drink than they had. I said I had quit alcohol, and it had been a good move. Soon, her friends decided that they had had enough for the day, and they left. They were all staying in the hotel.

I realised that the lady was flagging. She ordered another drink, and she had switched from white wine to red, but she didn't even touch it. Her conversation stopped; she had run out of steam. I still have that fleeting thought that perhaps I am boring, but I think the reality was that she had been drinking for several hours, and her body was making her feel tired so that she would stop drinking.

Before long, she decided she had to go to bed. They were heading off to MONA (the Museum of Old and New Art) tomorrow. She invited me along, but I am going to see big trees tomorrow: Huon pines.

I didn't last until the end of the music, either. I made my way upstairs, where I could still hear enough of the music to be able to identify the songs. It was very pleasant.

Friday 25 Aug 2023

The bus came to pick me up just before 7:45 am, but I was ready. Jack was the jovial driver. We had a full bus of eleven visitors plus Jack. It was an overcast day, which meant that the weather shifted continuously between heavy drizzle, cloudy, and sunny. We drove on the Huon Highway south of Hobart for the best part of two hours, and then we stopped at a tourist information centre and café where we got coffee.

The café was modern, all glass and steel and light, but across the road there was a quaint building that was the first office of the National Park guides, built in 1936. In those days the road was dirt, and this was a remote outpost. The building was memorable: what you might call the California chateau style, including two columns of small, round granite stones. I have an affection for such things. It was smartly painted in lemon yellow, with contrasts of dark brown.

The real feature of this place was the thermal springs. When you walked down into the gully, along a wooden walkway, you soon arrived at a shallow swimming pool, built in modern tiles. I put my hand in, and the water was quite warm. The air around me was probably about nine degrees. Perhaps if I came on my own, and my time was not measured by group norms, I would venture into the pool. It seemed to be a pleasant thing to do.

A short drive up the road took us to Hastings Caves, also called Newdegate Cave. To be honest, I had never heard of them, or perhaps I had but had not taken notice. I've never heard them talked about. So, in tourist language, you could say this is one of Tasmania's hidden secrets (this is not language I usually use). We went on a tour into the caves, and it is a spectacular place. They (and the thermal springs) were discovered by accident in 1916, by two young men.

There was logging taking place in the area, and a large tree had fallen down, and they had been tasked with cleaning up its branches so the timber could be assessed. It started to rain and they looked for shelter. What had happened was that the tree had fallen onto the entrance of the cave, so they found themselves in the shelter of the entrance.

They went a small way in, as far as the outside light penetrated. They call this the twilight zone. I think that is an amusing tag from later times. They were obviously excited because the next day, foregoing their daily schedule, they came back with lanterns and ropes. You think of all the things that were happening in the world at that time: Australia being involved in the First World War; whaling was still occurring – indeed, I had the thought that their lanterns could have been fuelled by whale oil. Apparently, it doesn't smoke much. There were known caves in other parts of Australia, especially the Jenolan Caves in New South Wales, known since the 1840s.

A few metres into the cave, there is a drop of about three metres. The men persevered, and went in for around a kilometre, but there were dangerous drops, and they did not go nearly as far as the caves extended. There is more than one route through; the length is over three kilometres, up and down. Today, the tourists route takes over an hour, but it takes about nine hours to go all the way through.

There are many steps, steel and wood with steel railings, but the overriding thing is the sheer beauty and wonder of the stalactites and stalagmites. The visiting group was about twenty-strong, and the guide was a lady. At one point she sang, in a lovely voice. The sound reverberated through the caverns. She said you can get married in the caves, for a certain price.

The guide described the unimaginably long time it takes for stalactites and stalagmites to form: they only grow about three millimetres per year, and the formations we were looking at were three and four metres high. Some of the stalactites were really thin, and were called straws. In the early days of tourism, you could break off a piece of stalactite and take it home: souveniring was welcomed. Nowadays the fine for doing that is over $10,000 and five years' gaol. People were naïve: childish enjoyment.

Your mind tries to imagine how long this cave took to form: millions of years, and all the other things that were going on at the time: the movement of continents, the rise and fall of oceans, erupting volcanoes, the birth of early humans and the arrival of Aborigines to what is now Tasmania. One tries to imagine the dynamics of a cave: the rainfall, the flow of water through the earth, the effect of floods within the cave, the leaching of tannin out of trees and its incorporation into the stalactites. The dynamics are all visible, but the scale is so far beyond ordinary life.

Apparently, said the guide, the Aborigines never lived in the caves, probably because of the steep drop just inside the entrance. Also, the lack of movement of air may have discouraged them. If they had lit a fire, they would have smoked themselves out. The temperature inside is constant, at around nine degrees all year, even when it is hot and sticky outside in summer. But there is not a lot of room: there are so many stalactites and stalagmites, there is not a lot of room for living.

One may wonder why the caves did not become popular, as the Jenolan Caves did. This may have been due to circumstances after 1916. The war was on, and then the Depression, and then another war, and it has taken quite a lot of work to make the caves safely accessible to visitors. But they are extraordinary, and it forces you to think about the planet from a different angle. As the guide said, "There is still so much we do not yet understand about the dynamics of the caves."

The Duke and Duchess of Kent came to visit Australia in 1927. They sailed out here on the ship HMS *Renown*, and their primary purpose was to open the new Parliament House in Canberra. While in Sydney, they took a steam train ride to Katoomba, and from there they went to visit Jenolan Caves. (The Duke became King George VI, and his wife was the lady we knew as the Queen Mother.) Jenolan Caves was already famous, and it was a huge and spectacular site. In contrast, Hasting Caves were a long way away and their public profile was overshadowed.

We drove back to Geeveston for lunch at the Kermandie Hotel, which was quite acceptable. The special moment was a rainbow across the waters of the Huon River. Rainbows in Tasmania are very broad: the bands of colour are very wide. They are also generally full, from end to end, but transitory. Thirty seconds after I had taken a photo of it, it was already fading.

Lunch was followed by another long drive, this time into the hills. Looking at country houses is always interesting. The houses here covered the spectrum from tidy to showy to decrepit. Some people love their gardens, and they have masses of flowers and everything is tidy. Some gardens are messy but abundant, and some are sparse, with little to garner attention.

Likewise, the houses can be super-tight, well-kept and recently painted, while others are run-down and surrounded by discarded machinery, some of it having been sitting in the grass for a generation. One house, the driver told us, was an attempt to create a castle, and the owner had been working on it for more than ten years. My impression was more of an Islamic temple than a medieval castle, but perhaps the creator's idea is not yet evident.

As we drove into the hills, it was more like where I used to live in Kyogle. Winding road, taller trees, occasional distant views across valleys. More occasionally, bubbling creeks with water that looked pristine fresh. We stopped at the site, Tahune Adventures, where a steel aerial walkway had been built, which they call an Airwalk. It was next to the Huon River. The walkway was very high, perhaps fifty metres at its highest, and maybe it was three hundred metres long, in three runs. Near the end was a section that was cantilevered out from the rest of the structure, so that you hovered over the river.

The structure was very solid. The only place where I could pick up movement was at the end of the cantilevered section, where you could feel the wind. In one sense, it evoked danger, but the quest for safety had practically eliminated any sense of danger. There is tension at work here: the yearning for a thrill, and the admonitions of the safety authorities and the lawyers. We live in a bureaucratically mature society.

There was disappointment brewing here. The main reason for my taking the tour was to see giant trees, and especially Huon pines. There were some tall trees, but they were mostly stringybark gums. Worse, most of the trees in this area had been burned out in the 2019 fires. Black was everywhere, despite the new growth. Many trees were dead, and there were piles of young trees on the ground that looked as if they had been smashed. It was shocking.

I don't think I saw a single Huon pine today. I did see some enormous trees in the Hastings Caves area. When you walked up to the entrance to the caves, you walked through a gully, and the trees were enormous. There were also some giant stumps of trees that had been chopped down long ago. The men would climb up to about three metres to start chopping, to get above the buttresses at the base, so all the stumps were about three metres high. Now they are covered with moss and the wood is rotting. It is a museum of Australian colonial rural activity.

There were young trees that were extremely tall as well, with straight trunks of, say, fifty metres, and trunks still slender, about 450 millimetres in diameter.

The bus made its way back to Hobart. Some people were sleeping. The journey into Hobart was circumlocuitous, because the driver was taking people back to various hotels. The bus went past the campus of the University of Tasmania, so I did get to see it. It is in its own little alcove. The driver said there was a noisy public debate about the university's proposed move away from this campus into the city, into a variety of buildings around the city, which would break up the concept of a campus.

Everything is worth a lot of money these days: real estate is expensive. People question why the university's governing body want to break up the campus and move the university into the city. I question why the governing body of an educational institution is playing real estate broker. There is a distinction between running a business and running an educational institution. One is about educating young people, and the other is about making money.

I know university governing bodies and their vice chancellors argue that the institution has to look to paying its own way in this competitive world. But that could also be merely an argument by someone who is more interested in the university as a business than as a vehicle for education. However, the very idea of higher education may have been superseded, displaced by the values of a capitalistic society. Degrees are just entry coupons into a primarily corporate way of life.

The value of knowledge has been attenuated. Courses are being continually shortened. What was once taught in fourteen weeks has had to be "delivered" in twelve weeks. After that, semesters were shortened to ten weeks. I have spoken to teachers who were well aware that, although the students were being awarded the same degree, the knowledge that was able to be included in the course has been progressively truncated: ruthlessly, and driven by external motivations, not the demands of the field itself.

One could argue that this is a good thing, because then you can create any number of higher degree courses: Master's degrees, Graduate Diplomas. Well, it must be good for business. This is the world we live in. There is an air of inevitability about it, and a voice that could be despair: what does it matter anyway?

I was dropped off at my hotel as the sun went down. It was not a rainy day, although it had rained. It was not a freezing day, although it had been cold. It was an illuminating day, as they all are.

I decided that I should eat dinner, and that I should "go out", having already eaten at the Shipwrights Arms. I found my way down the hill to Salamanca and had seafood linguini at a bar. It was quite nice, and nowadays many places have non-alcoholic beer. Then up the hill again to my hotel. I have concluded that there is usually little gain from hanging around bars at night. The sky was cloud-strewn, so there was little to be had of star-gazing.

50

Saturday 26 Aug 2023

Today is the day of Salamanca Markets. It is very large, and widely interesting. There may even be items that are of interest to buy. Also, it would be nice to see Claire Hansen again. The cover of one of my books, *Future*, features one of her pictures. I met her at her stall at the Salamanca Markets in October 2019.

Also today, I want to revisit the man with the antique maps, at his shop. I want to see if he has located the map by Findlay of Hobart's layout in 1854. And I want to go to see the Penitentiary again; I only walked past it the other day. I have new questions to ask that pertain to Edward Lewis and Sarah Crosby. But first, I want to go to the post office and post a package of books back home. I did not bring a large suitcase, and unfortunately, I have purchased some books.

I thought it would be smart to post books home. I have never done this before, and the idea is amusing. Will it be a costly exercise? Well, it's a question of what the alternatives are. I only have one suitcase and one backpack: one for checking-in, and one for carry-on luggage. They are both full.

My deliberations were a moot point. The Battery Point Post Office was closed, and when I checked online, I discovered that all post offices (in Tasmania, I guess) are closed on Saturdays. So, I will have to manage my luggage to Oatlands, where I am going tomorrow, and sort it out when I get there. I took the bag of extra luggage, mostly books, back to the hotel and set out for Salamanca Markets once more.

The markets were extremely large, all the way from Davey Street to Kelly's Steps, bigger than The Channon from my far-north-coast (New South Wales) days. I am more distant now, and I can think about the market stallholders more objectively. I wonder about longevity: is having a stall a temporary endeavour, or is it a lifetime passion? It takes a willingness to narrow your focus: I will make gin, or scarves, or meringues, or leather bags, or cleansing essences.

I imagine that people go through cycles with it. Do they doubt the value of what they are doing and question it? Are they obstinate, and resist this questioning? Are they disillusioned and unhappy? Or have they found some form of contentment? Are they happy doing what they do? Do they earn enough money to be happy with how they live? I have questions. Do I see answers on the stallholders' faces, in how they hold themselves and how they look at people (or shall we say "customers")?

I heard one young man say to his companion: "I don't need anything." I thought it was odd to hear that from a young man. I heard another young man say on the phone: "I just need some money in my credit card account." I actually heard that sentence twice today. The other time was a young lady saying on her phone: "I just need you to put some money into my credit card account." Those statements could be part of numerous scenarios; they certainly paint a picture of family dynamics, and understandings about expectations and responsibilities.

There was such a variety of items at the market, but I felt like the young man who said he didn't need anything. More practically, if I buy something, I have to transport it home to Sydney. But I did see some beautiful things. The ones that attracted me the most were ceramics: vases, bowls, mugs and other items by one craftsman. It was the vases that attracted me. They were of various shapes, and were smooth-skinned and bone-white in colour. But what stood out were the black threads running down the sides, twisted about like DNA helixes.

I asked the man what this was. He asked me whether I did pottery. My experience with pottery was a few afternoons on a pottery wheel about fifty years ago. He laughed gently. So, the answer was that, at a certain point in the firing process, he took the pots out of the kiln and draped wool from alpacas (he owned alpacas) down the side, then put the pots back in. The wool burned away, leaving it black. He pointed out that above the black threads you could see a pale smokiness, which was from the wool burning off in the kiln.

I will have to think of how I can bring things like this back to Sydney on future trips. They were truly gorgeous.

I looked up and down for Claire Hansen and her artwork. I love her pictures. I think they emanate soul, yet they are not cute or cloying. Some artists can draw/paint images that seek to evoke emotions, but they rely on childish beliefs. I thought Claire's work was grounded in the earth, but there was something deeper in it that was about joy. It could therefore be whimsical without being trivial or sentimental.

That's all I will say on that, because the talk can overtake the reality. At the same time, it seems that being an artist these days requires you to be quite literate: you have to be able to say something about your work ("the artist's statement"). I find that what Claire says about her paintings is quite literate. And I see dangers in the need for artists to be literate, because… the talk often overtakes the reality. Claire's work is grounded but light, knowing but not presumptuous.

There were other artists at the market. Most of them were not of interest to me. There are lots of things I am not interested in. I think that's a good thing, otherwise I might be overwhelmed with the world and all that's in it. It's best to put it the other way: what am I attracted to? There was one artist I liked. I thought her work was similar to Claire Hansen's, in style and perhaps in subject matter.

Sarah Elliott has a feminine perspective, with girls in most of her pictures, at least, the ones I saw. I think the style is magical realism, but I am on dangerous ground here: I pretend to no knowledge of art as a field of knowledge, much less art as a skill. The difference from Claire Hansen's work is that Claire's pictures have no elements of magic in them, no odd placements of object. In Sarah Elliott's work there was a tiny house in a rowing boat, and a girl as tall as a tree. In Claire Hansen's work, there may be just a boy and a girl standing under an umbrella, or a girl and a bicycle at the entrance to a park.

Disappointed with not finding Claire at the markets, I went to have a coffee, and looked her up online. Yes, she is still around. I found a painting of a girl in a library: how pertinent! I am thinking about libraries at the moment. I read a book on the history of libraries; I have my own library; I am going to book fairs and seeing if I can find books that I already have in my library (and I have been quite successful!).

In what Claire writes about that painting, she points to the childhood joy of the reader, getting lost in the stories in books. My perspective is of how books are connected with my thinking, and how new books extend my thinking, leading me in new directions. Often, they lead me in directions I have never thought about before. But I am still thinking about this business.

The hotel where I am staying has a library in its tiny loungeroom. It consists of seven books. I am sure it is a variable library: people leave books here, and they take them away with them. Three of the books are Mills & Boon romances, with suggestive pictures on the front covers: paintings, not photographs. One of the books is by Gunter Grass. I read one of his books years ago. This one, when I opened it, was in German. (The book I read, *The Tin Drum*, was, you might guess, in English.)

Somewhere in the last few days, around Hobart city, I saw a street library, which had about twenty books in it. I didn't try to catalogue its contents. I wonder about street libraries in Hobart: how do they fare in the weather?

Ah, I was going somewhere after the market. I was going to see the antique maps man. Oh, and I stopped to have a coffee. I had gone to a shop near the Salamanca Markets and ordered one, but after twenty minutes it hadn't come, and it didn't look like it was going to. No sense in demanding. I simply left, and found a shop near the antique maps shop where the staff were prepared to offer service to customers. I admit the first shop was busy, but the basic contract in a shop is that you provide a service.

Having been satisfied with coffee, I went to the maps store. It was closed. The man had said to ring the doorbell and he would come down, and I rang the doorbell, but after a reasonable interval he had not come down. Some days are smoother than others. No problem; I had more activities on my list. I walked in the direction of the old convict quarters: the Penitentiary on Campbell Street.

I arrived at 12:45 pm, and there was to be a tour at 1:00 pm. I booked for that, then I talked to the volunteer about my current quest: to figure out how Sarah Crosby and Edward Lewis met in Hobart in around 1852. Sarah was in and out of the Female Factory south of Hobart, going to numerous employers. One of those employers was the Police Magistrates Court.

Edward had been at Point Puer, and it closed down in March 1850, and he was sent to Hobart. At some point he was given a Ticket of Leave and he became a Special Constable. It seems that he could have stayed at the Penitentiary (colloquially known as the Tench). Up to a thousand convicts were housed here, and numerous guards. But the closer you get to certainty, things can get a little out of focus, and I still feel that. One person told me that the Police Magistrates Court was at the Tench, but this was only true after 1860. So, I needed my wits about me.

I went on the tour, and the lady was well-versed in the stories of the gaol, and of the building itself. And, she was most interested in the fact that I had two convict connections in my family in Hobart. We started the tour in the courtroom, and the guide confirmed that the Magistrates Court had operated here since 1860, and until well into the twentieth century. She described the bizarre history of the place, with a church built in three separate tiered parts, like the sides of a fold-out cube, and the minister (Church of England) delivered his sermon from the base of the three tiers. (The church was designed by John Lee Archer, the colonial architect.)

The reason for this was that two tiers were for the convicts, who were obliged to attend church on Sunday, while the third tier was for free parishioners who came from the local community. As if this was not bizarre enough, below the three tiers were solitary confinement cells, which were almost as small as coffins. The solitarily confined convicts felt no great sympathy for a minister's

55

rant on the need for sinners to repent of their sins, and they were cold and half-starved, so they would howl and moan during the service.

It is bizarre to think about people going about their ordinary lives and then attending a church service which put on display the travesty of the government's punishment and reform system. The prisoners, for the most part, and there were at times close to a thousand of them, had no interest in the service, and they would tell stories to each other, play cards, and even have surreptitious drinks (rum) under the pews.

When I think of a thousand people at church, I can only think of great occasions like the funeral of a major public figure, or a royal celebration of some sort, where the people are deferential and devout. It is hard to imagine it being an occasion where the church was forcing religion onto an unwilling mob.

My question was, was Edward Lewis stationed here as a special constable after he came to Hobart upon the closure of the boys' prison, Point Puer? Both the guide and the volunteer were certain that he did, that this would have been the place he was stationed. The Tench operated for a long time as the prisoners' barracks, and Edward was here in 1851-1852, so it fits.

I still have to get certainty about where the Police Magistrates Court was located around 1852, because that was where Sarah worked, and I also have to get certainty about where she would have stayed. This issue seems to exist at two levels: firstly, there is the conversational level, where you ask different people questions verbally, and get told what they know, or what documents to look at. Secondly, there is the level of documents and maps, and what is written down in different places.

Often, the people at a site know more than more qualified people working for various institutions. This is why I am going to Oatlands tomorrow: the local people have more interest in the things in their own locality, so they dig deeper into those questions.

I bought a book about convict places, called *Convict Places*, and it proves the same point. When a person looks at a question from their own perspective, they dig up things that are glossed over in other perspectives. Accordingly, a book on places will have details that other historians have ignored. The book has a section on Point Puer, for example, and it is clearer about some aspects that have been misunderstood over the years, such as the boys' daily routine. Examining this, you realise that, for all the noble wish to reform youth and educate them in a trade, there was precious little of the boys' day allocated to that purpose, and it was after dark, when they would have been tired.

I think Edward knew how to "fly below the radar". He had been a pickpocket, and the core skill there is to be invisible, to not be noticed. But when I said that to the guide, she said, "It didn't take much to be noticed. One cheeky remark and you could find yourself getting a dozen lashes." So, I don't know if Edward managed to get through his convict sentence unscathed.

In the early 1840s, two boys at Point Puer had murdered a guard, beaten him over the head with a hard object, and he had died without regaining consciousness. The two alleged murderers had been charged, and tried in the Hobart Supreme Court, and it was one of the rare occasions where the judge refused to find either of them guilty, because it was not clear who had done what. (The story is told by Steve Harris in *The Lost Boys of Mr Dickens*.)

However, the episode cast a shadow over Point Puer, and no doubt Edward heard about it when he arrived a couple of years later. Certainly, Edward's record card shows very little in the way of disciplinary actions during his time of servitude. He was given a Ticket of Leave and became a special constable.

The guide showed us the gallows, the place where people were hung. Many people had been hung at the Tench. And the guide talked about the life of Solomon Blay, the hangman. I suppose I would have some interest in this if it had involved someone in my family, but to me it was just sad: the end point of a brutal regime bolstered by appeals to the just Lord of all Creation.

When you travel, you come face to face with everything. What do I think about that period of time? Do I have answers that would have solved the social problems differently? Was everything inevitable, given the conditions of the time? Were all the contradictory forces equally necessary? Did they have to work themselves out through the bloody course of history?

One of the stories the guide told was about a group of convicts working on a road gang in the midlands, towards the end of the convict era. A commissioner came through doing an inspection of the state of things in the area. Many of the men in the road gang remembered this man from years ago as a cruel magistrate. They remembered his cruelty, and they rose up spontaneously and attacked him, killing him.

The guide said this was an exceptional case, but the convicts knew the difference between a magistrate who was "tough but fair", and a magistrate who was simply personally cruel, and used his position to exercise his penchant. They felt they had nothing left to lose anymore, and they got their revenge. Harsh times.

I remember that there were people around in this period of time who felt differently. An inspector who came to view the prison at the Tench viewed the solitary confinement cells and was horrified. He said they were unfit for humans under any circumstances. He agitated for the use of them to be stopped.

There were the Quakers who gave help to the Irish during the potato famine, and who had to tell the British Government in the end that the problem was too big, and the government should itself act to assist the starving Irish. There were the common folk of Hobart who protested at the conditions of the women at Cascades Female Factory, because so many babies were dying in the cold and damp conditions.

I think it's important to remove the monolithic idea that everybody thought the same way. They didn't. Some people saw that other groups were in misery, and that nothing good was going to come of perpetuating harsh conditions. Sarah and Edward survived. They met, they married, they had several children, including my great grandmother, Ellen Elizabeth Lewis.

I walked back into town, and past the Antique Prints and Maps shop again. Maybe he would be there. It was about 3:00 pm (Saturday). The door was open. He remembered me and said, "Oh, you were wanting that map of Hobart. I'll go up and see if I can find it." He was back down again in a few moments, with a large sheet of paper; I think it was A2 (420 x 594 mm). I had a close look. He brought me a magnifying glass.

While I was looking, I realised the map also showed Watchorn Street in 1854, and Edward and Sarah Lewis, recently married, were living there. It looked as if it had a row of houses down both sides of the street, a stark contrast to its present unattractive functionality. And they had had twins here, their first children: Sarah Ann and Mary Susannah.

In between, Gerard told me he had just put a bid on a print of a Tasmanian Aboriginal woman from the early 1800s. He said it was a page out of a book, and the picture had been coloured. The bid was around $100. The paper was water-stained and it looked to be in poor condition. He wanted to be able to make prints off it, and he doubted he could get it clean enough, so he decided to pass on it. I didn't realise you could clean up a print and be able to make prints off it, but he was well-versed in the options, and the steps to take. I felt respect for his expertise.

I said I was leaving Hobart tomorrow, but I was coming back later in the week, and could he make a copy of the Hobart map? He said he would. The last thing he said to me was: "Don't get obsessed about this!" It was a good thing to say, but I didn't expect it from him. He smiled and I laughed.

Finally, I was thinking about lunch. It was close to 4:00 pm. I have not had a proper meal of salmon since I have been in Tasmania, so I went looking for that. On the wharves, one of the piers had a restaurant that specialised in fish. That's where I went. I had a lovely meal of salmon: simple, grilled, with a salad. Then I walked back up to the Shipwrights Arms. This was my last night, so I had to think about packing, and whether everything I had would fit.

Sunday 27 Aug 2023

Up bright and early, packed successfully (meaning, I got everything to fit into my luggage), and I was out on the street in time to greet the taxi I had booked. He took me to the bus transit stop to go to Oatlands. Fortunately, I had done my homework. I had been on this bus before, in 2019, I think, and it was called the Grey Line. Now, it had merged with a bigger bus company, one that had buses in Europe, and its name was Kinetic. There are many times in our society where historical knowledge does you no good, because behind the scenes someone is thinking of how the business could be better (but still committed to your comfort and safety) and what would be a snappier name?

But the bus was magnificent. It was red, and quite new. It was smooth and shiny. It had seatbelts. It even had ports for charging your digital devices. I brought a book to read (on my phone), but I looked out the window instead. I don't come this way often, and it would be a shame to miss it because I was reading a book. Even if the book was about a Tasmanian lady, Edith Emery. She was born in Austria, and was caught up in Hitler's war, but afterwards she came to Tasmania to live. She was both a doctor and an architect: she was an unusual person.

It takes about an hour and a half to get to Oatlands from Hobart. The bus was rather full. People were going to Launceston and to places up along the northwest coast. Only two people got off at Oatlands, myself and another man. Oatlands is flat and the streets are wide. Then I saw that just about all the buildings (houses as well as public buildings) are made of sandstone, and many of them are quite ornate. This is most unusual for a small town. The brochures say the town has the most sandstone buildings (over one hundred) of any town in Australia. I had read that, but it wasn't until I saw all the buildings that it sank in.

My check-in time at the accommodation was 2:00 pm, but it was only just after 11:00 am. I wasn't sure what I would do about checking in. I found Robinson's Cottage. The place next door, a bar called "The Imbibers", was attached, with a verandah down the side, so I was bold enough to leave my bags on the verandah and dawdle up the street to see if I could find a café for having some coffee. I hadn't gone too far when I saw a café on the other side of the road. I knew it was open because there was a billboard out on the footpath. The door was closed. I figured that's how it was in winter.

The café was a light-framed building joined to a solid sandstone house. Off to the side of the café was a garden, with a few chairs and tables, obviously for the sunny days. I opened the door and went in. The lady was old, probably in her seventies (I say this with amusement now, given that that is exactly what people would say of me with my grey hair). She had a compartment on the counter with an assortment of cakes that you would hope to find in a good café but probably wouldn't, not in a small rural town. I chose hummingbird cake and cappuccino.

She told me she had been here twenty years, and that she had moved down here from Leura, in the Blue Mountains in New South Wales. I could imagine that. She told me they get snow in Oatlands about as often as they get snow in Leura. I've never lived in a place that gets snow. That's okay; it's nice to hear about it from others. I told her of my quest to find my great great grandmother. She told me to go to the Museum and History Room. She said they have done lots of research, all of them volunteers, and they would keep me there until they had answered all my questions!

Before I went there, I went back to where I had left my suitcase. The Imbibers was now open, and a cheery man was there, Nathan. I asked him about getting access to Robinson's Cottage. He sorted it out and took me around to the room; most helpful. He also gave me the rundown about food tonight in Oatlands. There is none. Nothing is open. There is a supermarket; I think he was implying I could purchase something there during the day.

However, I thought I saw a solution. I had managed to have a meal of salmon the other day in Hobart, but I had not yet had a cheese platter of Tasmanian cheeses. And I thought this place did

61

just that, so I asked him if he could prepare me a cheese platter that I could have this evening. This was indeed a possible solution; Nathan was happy to oblige. He said to come back and see him during the afternoon, after I had looked around and been to the History Room, and he would have one ready for me.

The bar was well-stocked with spirits. I thought that he might encourage me to have a drink, so I said it was funny standing there, because I had given up drinking alcohol two years ago. When you make a statement like that, you never know where the conversation will go. But he answered straight away, with the most unexpected answer. He said, "Nor do I. I have given up."

He was probably around forty, so I wondered what prompted him to give up, and I asked him. Once again, he was frank. He said, "I am not a nice person when I'm drunk. I might be having a good time, but other people aren't. The worst parts of my Irish and Aboriginal ancestry come out."

I was surprised at his frankness, but I thought it was laudable. I told him that I gave up because I found myself drinking more, and drinking more frequently, and I thought it was no good for me. And I am getting older, and I always thought I would stop drinking one day, so why not today? So I did stop, just like that, two years ago. And it is perfectly fine.

He said, "Do you drink lots of tea? I do, and all sorts of teas. I have become quite the teetotaller! Different teas for different times of the day; chamomile at night."

I said that Japanese green tea was one of my favourites. It has roasted rice in it.

Nathan had one last comment about alcohol: "It's poison, you know." I was surprised to hear this remark from him, but I had heard the statement before. After I had resolved to stop drinking alcohol, I had acquired a book called *The Alcohol Experiment* by Annie Grace. It contains a chapter called "Is alcohol really poisonous and addictive?" In the chapter, she describes how alcoholic drinks contain ethanol, and how that affects your body. She paints a dire picture.

She is quite blunt: alcohol is a poison. My own stance on this is a bit more nuanced. The concept of homeopathy is that some poisons, in miniscule doses, may actually be good for healing us. This is not my argument, because obviously people don't drink alcohol in miniscule doses. The point is that it opens up the recognition that it is not a simple yes/no question; there are nuances, there is a spectrum.

There is another consideration. At the other end of the spectrum, some foods may be poisonous in excessive amounts. For example, I heard of a case where a man died from eating too many carrots. People can get obsessive about the health properties of particular foods, and this man expected miracles from carrots. But carrots contain Vitamin A, which is poisonous in large amounts.

This feeds into the idea of drinking in moderation. But, I suspect that many people are a bit too casual about what that means. To reach a decision for yourself, I think you have to consider the full range of options, and be prepared to be stern (that is, honest) with yourself.

I don't claim to be an authority on health or biology. My focus is more on my state of mind, and how to foster what I would call positive consciousness (tomorrow I might have a different expression for it). I would say that many people might find Annie Grace's book helpful. The essence of Nathan's story, for me, was how he recognised the problems with his social behaviour, how he changed his habits (in relation to drinking alcohol), and how he recognises the positive change in his consciousness.

Some people might argue that you don't have to give up alcohol altogether; you just have to learn moderation. I don't argue with that. I don't preach, and I don't make rules for others. I made the decision I felt I should make for myself. I feel it was a good decision.

With the arrangement for my dinner in place, I made my way down the street to the Museum and History Room. I told the lady, Patricia, my story, about how Sarah Crosby had been brought here straight from the ship, the *St Vincent*, when it reached Hobart Town in April 1850. And how she worked for Charles Sutton at an inn. But after three months she committed an indiscretion: she was found in bed with a man, after 9:30 at night. She was sent back to Hobart, to Cascades Female Factory. And that was the end of her association with Oatlands.

Patricia first looked for Sarah Crosby. There were a lot of convicts, men and women, that were sent to Oatlands, and they had created files on as many of them as they could, and their subsequent families. But there was nothing on Sarah. This was not surprising, as she was not here long, and she formed no ties that I am aware of.

Next, I was interested in Charles Sutton: who was he? Had he come out from England as a free man to start a business in the colony? What was the history of his connection with the inn? And what was known about the hotel? I didn't even know its name.

There was a file on Charles Sutton, including a copy of a very large sheet of paper which was the sales contract for a parcel of land, a town block, in the twenty-second year of His Majesty's reign. Neither of us knew which year this was. Charles Sutton was buying the land. But it wasn't this I was interested in. Then we came to pages that told us a bit more about Mister Sutton. He had been a convict, and he had stolen a sheep: in the colony; it was not the reason for his transportation. He married, and there were children. He died in 1855.

In the late 1840s, he obtained the licence for the inn, and there were about twelve people who lived in, or were staying at, the inn. This was great. I was building up a picture of the man. Next, I wanted to get a picture of the hotels in the town, to find the name of Sutton's inn, and to see how it fitted into the history of hotels in this town. There was another folder on the town's inns/hotels. It was a large folder.

There had been many hotels in the town, but Charles Sutton's was not insignificant. It was called the Wilmott Arms, and later it was the Midlands Hotel. There was information about all of this, just what I wanted. There were two typed pages in particular, with information about the Wilmott Arms, and Patricia said she would photocopy them. But a moment later, I heard the malfunction beeps from the machine; it had jammed. She asked me if I would look at it.

I do have experience of paper jamming in photocopiers, so I know the initial steps to take. I managed to find out how to open up the machine, and I carefully took the paper out. However, I tried the Copy button three more times, and the machine was determined to jam. I managed to get a print of the two pages I needed, but I said they would need to get a technician in, because he could figure out why the paper was jamming.

Eventually, I looked around the museum. It was a well-stocked museum, on all aspects of ordinary life over the last hundred years. This town has managed to keep so much! An adjoining building was a replica of a modest, two-roomed settler's cottage, nicely furnished, down to the wallpaper in the bedroom. The fireplace had a cast-iron fuel stove. Back inside, Patricia pointed out the bootmaker's workshop. It had several machines, for stitching the leather, and shoe lasts for the shoes as they were being made. Some of the machines I had not seen before.

In my whole family tree, there is only one bootmaker; it was Edward Lewis's son. He had been a troubled youth who had got into trouble several times. He had beaten people up, including punching two women. He had been in a gang that beat up drunks and stole from them. Eventually he ended up in gaol. (This was in New South Wales.) However, in gaol he had learned the trade of boot-making. He never got into any further trouble with the law. I like to think that he straightened himself out.

I had never seen what a boot-maker's workshop looked like. I just had an image of a bootmaker with a shoe on a last, but this is mostly for making repairs, not for actually making the shoes. I have a better feel now for what they do, and what their environment must feel like to work in. I imagine the son working on a pair of boots, thinking about his life now as compared to his angry young days.

However, his death certificate indicates that he drank heavily, so I imagine that the young-man anger channelled itself into sad drinking. I don't know the reasons. In family history, sometimes you get so close, but it is still so far.

There are some buildings in Oatlands that are locked and not staffed, but you can pick up a key that lets you in, so you can tour around by yourself, letting yourself in and out. That implies a lot of trust. I think it also sets a tone in the town, as if to say, "This is a town of trust."

I spent the rest of the afternoon strolling around. I went into two of the locked buildings that had the key to get in: the Commissariat and the Supreme Court. This town and Launceston were the only places outside Hobart where the death sentence could be carried out. The same hangman used to come up here to carry out the sentences. It was Solomon Blay, as at the Tench. When he was travelling, other people did not like to have him in their carriage. The Supreme court overlooked the town's nearby lake. It was over the road from the gaol.

The gaol still has a huge wall, although it has been reduced from over twenty-feet high to about thirteen feet (alright: six metres to four metres). The wall runs around a whole block, maybe a hundred metres long on each side. It is still imposing. There is one two-storey building left, which used to be the warden's home, so it looked down into the gaol yard. The executions were carried out in Oatlands, and up until the 1850s they were public, so people would come and watch. The lives of eighteen men ended this way.

Part of the gaol yard became the town's swimming pool. Life in some places can be an odd business.

When I visited Cascades Female Factory a few years ago, there was an exhibition in the Matron's Cottage of bonnets that current Tasmanian women had made in commemoration of individual women convicts from the period up to 1853, when transportation to Van Diemen's Land ended. The style of the bonnets was that of the bonnets the convict women wore, and the convicts' names were embroidered on the bonnets.

I think the wearing of the bonnets was an attempt to make them demure. For some women, this did not work; they were street

66

fighters. They had determined to be defiant until their last breath. Babette Smith's book, *Defiant Voices* (NLA Publishing, 2021), depicts some of these women. They were formidable.

This time when I went to Cascades Female Factory, the exhibition had gone. This was understandable, it was an exhibition, it was there for a specific duration. But inside the Supreme Court, here at Oatlands, after I had used my special key to get inside, there were some of the bonnets. It made me think: exhibitions can assume a life of their own, and be seen by different audiences. Occasionally, some of those people would be the same!

I also visited Callington Mill, which is now a distillery making single-malt whisky. On the site is a windmill, styled on windmills in Lincolnshire, and built in 1837. It has been restored to functionality, and it is capable of milling flour as it used to. On this note, the Commissariat which I visited contains a wood-fired oven which was built after the convict days were over, and at one stage it was the place where townspeople came to get their bread. It could bake sixty loaves. The commentary at the site observed that it was fitting that the Commissariat, which held all the town's provisions securely during the convict days, and which was guarded night and day, once again became the source of food for the town.

The distillery itself is housed in modern premises, very stylish, with a dining room for many people.

When I came back to The Imbibers, Nathan was busy preparing my cheese platter. He told me that he and his partner had started the business just at the start of the COVID pandemic, and it was difficult to get food in from distant places. They decided that they would only sell local food, from within about fifty kilometres of Oatlands. Accordingly, all the food, and the alcoholic drinks, come from local suppliers. In particular, my cheese and bread platter consisted entirely of local cheeses.

It was delicious.

Monday 28 Aug 2023

My day was unplanned, but I am not daunted by this. I have done it before. I had nothing for breakfast except a cup of green tea, but that is quite fine. I don't live by the credo that "breakfast is the most important meal of the day". In fact, I think fruit may be the best thing to eat in the morning. Heavy food just weighs your stomach down from the start. As long as you can get something later in the morning.

I had read through the guest book to see what previous occupiers of this "contemporary apartment" had to say about it. It was mostly complimentary, although some people had got upset about the remote control for the television not working. I haven't watched the television, so I don't know about that. But several of the visitors had remarked on how wonderful the shower was.

The shower was roomy; that's the first observation. The showers I have been in on this trip merit no remarks; they served the purpose, that's all. One was too small: I kept bumping into myself. But this Robinson's Cottage shower was generous with space. I like space.

Then, the shower-head was a large square, from which water ran like a waterfall: long, heavy falls of water which felt soft and replenishing. So, I agree with the other visitors. Most of the visitors had booked in merely as a place to stay between Launceston and Hobart, but they immediately realised they were in a place where you could happily spend quite a lot of time. The accommodation itself was cosy, and the town deserved time for exploration.

Satisfied with the shower I had, I went out to get morning tea. I went back to the Vintage on High café, seeking coffee and some little food. She had on offer what she called fruit toast, but that really undersold what arrived. It was a slab of fruits, which had been mixed in a bowl with a very minor amount of flour, and then put in the oven for a while. It was a delight.

I told the lady that I had been successful on my trip to the History Room yesterday, and had found out information on Sarah's employer, the publican. And I asked her about the large device that stood in the café. She told me it was a coffee grinder from a coffee supplier in the old days. It had an ornate funnel at the top, and a large wheel, more than a metre in diameter, and it was turned by a handle. It owed more to aesthetics than to industry.

It was time to fulfil my quest to post a parcel of books back home. I took the parcel to the post office. Inside, it had that small-town feel. There were only a couple of people in there, but they had that easy familiarity, as if they passed each other frequently through the day. I told the lady I was posting a parcel to myself, and she was amused but supportive. I chose a post bag, and she took over the process of easing the books into it.

I put the sender's address as "c/- Oatlands Post Office". Two days later, I got a text message saying that the parcel had arrived. I thought that was impressive, even a bit too impressive. When I got home, my son told me it had actually arrived on Thursday afternoon, so the text message was a little premature.

Mission accomplished. I walked back down the street, past the antiques store, with its crazy profusion of olden-days memorabilia. I might have thought about it differently if I had lived closer, but I was resistant to falling in love with anything. It was a question of being able to transport it home. There were a few items of nice furniture. Mostly they had crockery, lots of crockery. It was crowded, and I didn't venture too far because the aisles were very narrow, and I feared that I would bump into things and break them. As I was looking, the store-keeper walked through to the footpath out front, eating a banana.

I got the impression he had inherited this place, or perhaps his wife had; yes, that was more likely. He gave the impression that he had picked up a few clues about the contents of the shop, such as which items might sell for a good sum of money, but he had no personal attachment to, or understanding of, any of it. I know we

69

shouldn't make assumptions, but so often it is quite useful to make assumptions about people.

Moving on up the street, I had another look at the Midlands Hotel with its surrounding construction fence. I realised I had been too quick yesterday: there were two parts of the building, one brick, and one stone. Obviously, the stone part was the early part, and the brick part had been added, I would think, in the twentieth century. It had a "fifties" feel about it (1950s), and someone had told me there was no heritage order on it. The brick part was far larger than the stone part.

I was told that the person who owned Callington Mill, the windmill and distillery, owned this building as well. There were supposedly plans to develop it, but the progress was intermittent and unconvincing. I got photos of the stone part.

I took photographs of more of the stone houses. I walked close to Lake Dulverton and found a sign which talked about it. I was dismissive yesterday, describing it as little more than a shallow swamp. The feature of the lake is that it is a habitat for many birds. I saw many swans, and I also saw many cygnets (I had to remind myself that baby swans are called cygnets): about twenty of them in a group; I should say, flock.

The other thing I noticed was that when I was close to the lake, I always heard crickets. I found one of the many plaques that give information about the town. This one was about the lake. It said that in the mid-twentieth century, many people in the town kept their own dairy cow. For a payment to the council of ten shillings a year, the cow wore a tag, and was allowed to roam the streets. At dusk, they had to be collected, whereupon they were taken home to be milked, and they were locked up overnight. After being milked again in the morning, they were freed to wander the streets again.

The other thing the cows did was to walk into the lake, right in until only their head and the top of their spine, and their tail, were visible. They gained some kind of nourishment from the lake. That is a memory of older people even today.

Addendum

Later, I read that Lake Dulverton had completely dried up in 1993, and it had stayed that way until 2010, when heavy rains filled the lake again. The maximum depth of the lake is three metres.

I walked into the yard of Callington Mill. It is very tidy, and numerous buildings are open for viewing: stables, a room where flour was kept, a room where barrels of liquor were kept and, of course, the mill itself. Almost immediately, a man came up to talk to me. He had a strange story to tell. He was dressed in uniform, black tee-shirt with a motto embroidered on it. He told me he had been the miller from about 2010 to 2019, but the mill doesn't perform any work anymore, and he has nothing to do. However, he was kept on, because the mill had to be kept functional.

I had heard bits of the mill's story from several people. From the 1970s, plans had been made to restore the mill. It had been run-down; it didn't even have sails. The original mill had been designed on the plans of one in Lincolnshire, England, and built in 1837. It seems that Lincolnshire was famous for having windmills. One assumes this was because it is on the coast of the English Channel.

There was a succession of government grants, from both State and Federal governments, for example in 1988, the Bi-centennial year. (I remember this year, because I wrote my first book, on the history of Kyogle (far north coast of New South Wales), on a Federal Government grant in 1988: *Places in the Bush*)

Several million dollars went into the restoration of the mill, which included trips to and from England by expert millers. The man in the tee-shirt knew milling, but he had had to learn how to mill flour for artisan millers, who had particular requirements, for example, for wholemeal and for sourdough bread. But in about 2019, it was decided that the mill was not viable, although the previous thinking was that tourism would not be enough to keep the mill going; it would need to have a functional role, that is, actually grinding flour for bakers.

I asked the man if he was happy doing nothing, and he said, in strong terms, no, he was not.

I went into the distillery. Given that I do not drink alcohol, and I never liked whisky, I didn't come to sample a tasting. However, I thought my son, the one that lives at home with me, might like a nice bottle of whisky. Choosing one was not easy, because I am hardly a judge between this one and that one, but I did make a choice, and left with a little black bag containing the prize.

My next quest was to visit the churches. There was a Church of England, a Catholic church, and a Uniting church. There were also graveyards. Did I need to go to a graveyard? Some people think I visit graveyards simply because I like looking at graves. There is an element of truth in that, but I usually have a more specific purpose in mind. There are no relatives in my family who are buried in Tasmania, except for Mary Ann Crosby, the baby that Sarah had while she was a convict. I don't know when or where that baby died, and many such babies were just buried *en masse* on the hillside behind Cascades Female Factory.

But I did have someone to find at Oatlands: Charles Sutton, the publican who had been Sarah's employer in 1850. I knew he had died in 1855, and I wanted to see his grave, because sometimes you find out things there that you don't learn from documents. He was Church of England, so I needed to go to their cemetery. However, the Catholic Church was close, so I decided to visit it first.

The Catholic Church was down a side street, not very far, but around a corner, so I had not seen it at first. It was, of course, made of stone. As I walked into the yard, I saw that there was a person in the dwelling near the church, sitting near a window. I guessed it was the presbytery (but at the moment, I was caught between religions; I knew it wasn't a vicarage, or a manse, but was it a rectory?). I instantly knew that the person would come out to see me.

Moments later, an elderly man came out and walked up to me with a giant key in his hand. He smiled, introducing himself as

Father Edmond. I introduced myself. He asked me if I wanted to see inside the church, because he had the key. He held the key up laughingly, because it was so big. Yes, I did want to see the church.

He asked me if I was interested in architecture, because the church was designed by Augustus Pugin, an English architect who designed the interior of the Palace of Westminster in Westminster, London, and its iconic clock tower which houses the bell known as Big Ben. He was also responsible for the revival of a Gothic style of medieval village churches. In Australia, there were several churches designed by him, but only a few which are still intact (Brisbane, Berrima, Sydney and Oatlands). Note, Pugin never visited Australia.

I said that my interest was family history, and my great great grandmother, who was Irish, had been a convict in Oatlands. I thought she might have gone to church here.

He told me that he was not the parish priest, but was here as a hermit for the time being. I don't know if he meant to surprise me, but I was interested in the idea of someone professing to be a hermit. I learned about one hermit when I was researching for the book I wrote on the history of Kyogle.

Paddy O'Dell had come to Kyogle in the 1920s and he lived in the bush at Collins Creek for several decades. He was described by the locals as a hermit. He lived alone, occasionally doing work for local farmers to earn some money. He occasionally went into town to get supplies. One old farmer remembered him, and told me he would get the bus, but he never sat inside the bus; he always stood at the door, on the bottom step. But I don't know if Paddy ever described himself as a hermit.

And I know that there is a tradition in the Catholic Church of hermits, although I didn't know that anyone today would attest to that label. But in Sydney, near where I live, there is a Benedictine Monastery, and I think of the monks there as being hermits. The order has an internal life; they are not running a school or a social welfare agency. I could probably arrange to go there if I wanted some quiet time in that kind of company. It's not out of the question.

73

In the present day, there is a hermit living on the Hawkesbury River, just a few kilometres north of me in Sydney. A few years ago, before all the local newspapers disappeared forever, there was an article about him. He lived in a cave not far from a town, and not far from the banks of the river. He seemed to have a cosy set-up, and to be prepared to talk to people. But nowadays I realise that a newspaper article is just a story by a journalist; it tells a story, but the perspective is what the journalist wants to convey.

I try to be honest, careful, and open.

Our problem is that, as a society, we have no frameworks for making sense of hermits except for social, psychological or economic factors. The Chinese poet, Xie Lingyun (4th century AD), wrote: "All my life I yearned to be a hermit, but was too weak. I went astray. Now, at last, I can embrace the Light of Innermost Self." Which is to say: there are other perspectives.

But we didn't talk about hermits. He jangled the giant key in the lock and opened the imposing door into the church. I told Father Edmond that I was looking for information relating to Sarah Crosby, an Irish girl of seventeen or eighteen who had been sent to Oatlands to work at the inn in 1850. She was definitely Roman Catholic, and I wondered whether she might have attended church at Oatlands.

I supposed it depended on Charles Sutton, her employer, who would have been Church of England (I have reasons for thinking this), but he may have felt sorry for her, and he may have thought it best to allow her to do so. I had read the sign out in the yard of the church, which informed me that when Sarah was there (April to July 1850), the church was not open; it was still being constructed. It opened in late February 1851, by which time Sarah had gone. Later, I read that the foundation stone for the church was laid on 9 April 1850, the same week that Sarah arrived at Hobart.

The Father told me something useful, very soon in our conversation. If a church was being built, then most certainly Mass would be celebrated each Sunday somewhere in the vicinity of the church building. If Mister Sutton had been agreeable, the young Irish girl could certainly have attended Mass. I thought of that in terms of whether Sarah retained her faith throughout her life. But as I told the Father, she is buried in the Catholic section at Rookwood, so I think she retained her allegiance and would have wanted to attend Mass when she lived here.

When we went inside, he showed me a plaque which had the name of the priest, Father Martin McRohan. He had been the priest here from the beginning, and he stayed for about thirty years. (We were sort-of sure about the spelling; the writing on the plaque was ornate. I thought it was amusing that his name incorporated my surname and the name of one of my sons.)

We talked for over an hour about the church, faith, society today, and philosophical questions. It was pleasant, as well as being a dance, because I am de-institutionalised, and he was of the flock, at the age of eighty-one. He was at the behest of the church, happily, doing, as he perceived it, God's work. I left the church (Anglican) over fifty years ago because I saw it as a dependency, and I wanted to stand on my own two feet. Quintessentially, that meant earning my own living, not being dependent on the church to do that for me (yes, it had been suggested to me that I become a minister).

I danced around that question, too. I told him I had grown up in the Church of England, but left it at that. In Hobart, I was walking near St David's Cathedral, and realised that St David's had been the name of the church where I had grown up. Recently, I went to a Buddhist meeting in Sydney. It was in a shiny new building, and there were about five hundred people there, mostly Chinese (although I think, Taiwanese). A lady spoke to me, and asked me about my alignment (or some other words to that effect), and I said I did not belong there.

She was sweet, and she said that I did indeed belong there, and I realised my phrasing was inadequate. I could have said I was de-institutionalised. That would have been closer to the truth. When I am being blunt, saying I am a non-joiner is correct. To the priest, I could have said that I do not belong to any organised religion. It's difficult. I could say I am a loner, which would have toyed with his description of himself as a hermit.

The Father's conception, I think, was simple: there is religion, and there is the secular world. The implication is that if you have left the church, you have rejected any notion of spirituality. This is quite apart from the problems that all organised religions have had with power-based sexual abuse of parishioners and children. I think that we have to recognise that all institutions are susceptible to such abuse, not just religious ones. Schools are one example. Inappropriate sexual behaviour is not a religious issue; it is an institutional issue.

There were many potential issues in our conversation that I thought would only trample on divisive ground. We should explore what was productive. This is not avoidance; it was recognition that neither of us had raised sexual abuse, and there were many other issues we might discuss. That's what we were doing.

He talked about it being pleasing that the different churches were now in conversation with each other, and there was no more acrimony between them. I said that it was productive to seek common ground. He corrected me. He thought "common ground" was a useful expression, but it was really a matter of people finding direct experiences they could both relate to. I liked that.

He talked about the nature of femininity and masculinity, and how they seemed to be confused these days. I had to talk with pauses, because I had not talked to someone of his persuasion for many years. He had been an army chaplain at one point, he had taught young men studying to become priests, and he had taught in military colleges. His point was that masculinity had to retain some sense of tenderness, and that the great generals had this quality.

His story was about a young man in the army during wartime, and young soldiers were suddenly realising that the future was extremely uncertain, and they should seize the offer of tenderness that was within their reach. One young man had a girlfriend, but he had been putting off proposing to her. He resolved that he would ask her as soon as possible to marry him, and he made a request of his sergeant to give him time off to go and propose to her.

The sergeant laughed and refused. The soldier said he wanted to make the request of the next higher officer in the chain of command, and this continued, with repeated refusals, until he obtained a meeting with the general. He was warned that if he met with the general to pursue his request, he would be severely reprimanded.

The crux was that he spent half an hour with the general, and the general gave him permission to go and ask his girl to marry him. They obviously had a good conversation. The lesson of the story was that an exceptional leader retains a sense of the importance of tenderness. Masculinity must incorporate this quality.

I accept the story and its lesson. There are similar lessons (insights) in the *Tao Te Ching* and the *I Ching*.

I reflected (without voicing it) that although my outlook has shifted away from the church, there are moments of resonance. I am not sorry I left the church and found my own way. I said, in response to his story, that my conception of masculinity and femininity is this: and I waved my hand in the air to trace the infinity sign. I said, each contains the other, for both men and women, and there must be a balance attained between them.

I am not sure that it made sense to him, but one never knows. I have to say what comes out of my perspective. We were not competing; we just came from rather different perspectives. He was a hermit inside the Catholic Church, and I am a non-joiner, which doesn't tell you anything except something in the negative. The conversation reinforced my sense of my need to leave the structure of the church. I could not have thought freely inside its structure or, for that matter, any structure.

Nevertheless, it was a good conversation to have. It was a kind of ecumenical exercise. In the end, however, such conversations can become mere philosophical posturing. It's hard to stay anchored in the heart when you are jousting intellectually. The Buddhists and the yogis say to meditate, and the essence of this is to stop thought, but who are you when there is no thought? How are you different from an animal? What is the nature of consciousness: this awareness without thought?

That was a conversation it might have been too difficult to have with Father Edmond. Not that he or I were incapable of it, but perhaps we both had too many obstacles to navigate. We accumulate so much mental furniture in our lives.

I walked up to the top of the hill to where the Uniting church was. They won the peak position: the Catholics and the Church of England are both in the lowlands. I eventually discovered that this Uniting church had been Presbyterian; the information plaque didn't say. Sometimes people want to leave the past behind. It was a nice church, too. The stonemasons were kept busy in Oatlands.

I don't understand why the church was either Presbyterian or Methodist. Presbyterian implies Scottish, and Methodist implies Cornish. I would imagine that most settlers here were English, especially in the time of the convicts. I would need to know more of the history of this place before I could answer this question.

Later, when I bought the book, *Oatlands*, it confirmed that the church had initially been Presbyterian. In my family tree there is a family of Scots (mother, father and several children) who migrated to Melbourne in the early 1840s. They were Presbyterian. The Scots were emigrating in a steady stream at this time. Accordingly, some of them must have come to Van Diemen's Land as well.

Another aspect I did not understand at this church was the absence of a graveyard. The church was on a large site, which included a large house for the minister, and there was ample unused ground around the church. Why was there not a graveyard here? Even the small Uniting church in my suburb in Sydney has its own graveyard, dating from the 1880s. As ever (happily), there are more questions than answers. We lurch and stumble towards understanding. Perhaps Presbyterians were buried in the "General Cemetery"....

There was an interesting story on the plaque at the Uniting church. The church had to be rebuilt after a storm blew down the steeple of the original building in August 1858. The steeple had been ninety-five feet high (29 metres), and in its fall it had smashed the church. However, Mister Wilson (whoever he was) was generous, and donated money to rebuild the church, and the job was done rapidly.

I had lunch at the Kentish Hotel. It was good. After that, I visited the Church of England, St Peter's, another fine example of the stonemasons' skill. I thought it was evocative that the Catholic Church should be St Paul's and the Church of England should be St Peter's. Who makes these decisions? St Peter's was built (with the help of convict labour) in 1838. In 1850, when St Paul's was being built and Father Martin McRohan was the first priest, the Reverend William Dry was minister of the Church of England. Did the two of them discuss the names of their respective churches?

A graveyard surrounded the Church of England, with some very old graves and some recent ones. There was also a memorial wall where the ashes of people who died in recent times were kept. I wondered how that works, because there certainly isn't a crematorium in town. I suppose cars solve everything, and bodies are taken to Hobart for cremation.

I looked at some of the graves, because I do, but there was a sign with some important information. Up until the late 1850s, Church of England people had been buried next to the Catholic Cemetery at the end of Stanley Street. So, any early burials of Church of England people would probably not be near the Church of England church, but out of town.

It was Charles Sutton's grave that I wanted to see. I knew he had died in 1855, so he had to be in the old cemetery. My next destination was there. It was on another side road, Stanley Street. I walked. And I walked. I expected it to be within a couple of hundred metres of the main road, but it was well over a kilometre away. Why? Usually, the cemetery is in town or very close to town.

I wonder if it had something to do with the fact that there were grand plans for Oatland. It was going to be the administrative centre of the midlands of Tasmania. When the initial plans for the township were drawn up, hundreds of town lots were proposed. It never came to be. Growth stalled early on. Perhaps, if the town was going to be large, the cemeteries would have to be further out.

I did eventually arrive. There was a sign, and a gate suitable for the entry of carts. It was closed up, but there was a pedestrian gate with a bolt, so I could get in easily. There were sheep. The cemetery was a sheep paddock. There was sheep poo everywhere. I stepped carefully. There were also lambs, many young lambs. This was a first for me. The best parallel I could think of was Clunes cemetery on the far north coast (of NSW), where I drove up onto a ridge, and the gate was shut; you had to open and close the gate when you drove your car in, to prevent cows from roaming into the cemetery. But there were no cattle there at the time.

I had a quest, so I started looking at graves. There was nothing to indicate what religion people were. Perhaps they were all Church of England? In the distance I could see a crowded graveyard, so that must be the modern Catholic cemetery. I felt that I was in the right place. Some of the gravestones were unreadable, which was no surprise. I had to be ready for disappointment. I thought that Charles Sutton's grave would be prominent, because he was a publican, and he would have considered himself to be important, whether or not other people thought so.

I didn't look at all the graves; I concentrated on the larger and more impressive ones. After about five minutes, I came across a tomb which was a large sandstone rectangular prism above ground, about one and a half metres high and two metres long. The underneath had subsided, and some of the foundations had fallen into the hole. The top had moss all over it. I walked all around it, and saw that there was writing on one side only. Then I got close to look at the writing. It was Charles Sutton, with his date of death written on the left of the stone, and the right-hand part of the stone was a plea for his wife to love his children after his death:

"Sacred to the memory of Charles Sutton, who departed this life January 8th 1855, aged 54 years. Farewell, dear wife, my life is past, thou loved me faithful 'til the last. Grieve not for me, nor sorrow make, but love my children for my sake."

I don't know what kind of man Charles Sutton was, but there were other things he could have said on his gravestone. This was touching. He was fifty-four, so he must have been born in 1800 or thereabouts. The words on the tomb are his words, and it is a lament for his wife and children. With that, I can track through and find the circumstances of his life.

I have learned so far that he had been a convict, but I don't know when he was transported or what his crime had been. And I knew he had had one child, a son, but "love my children" infers that there was more than one child. There is always more work to do.

I walked up to the modern Catholic cemetery, and I had to climb over the fence that was there to keep the sheep from wandering off. The first grave I looked at was close to the gateway, and it was for a man who had died after falling from the steeple of the church. When you think that the church is the house of God, that seems to be a tough way to go. I looked at some other graves, but my work for the day was done.

I walked back to town, along the edge of the shallow lake this time, and went back to the Kentish Hotel. I had decided that the answer to tonight's meal was to buy something there. I purchased a piece of vegetable quiche, which turned out to be very acceptable. I even bought a piece of pecan pie for dessert: a treat.

It is a full moon tonight, the second full moon this month, so it is called a blue moon: for amusement only; it is not blue. The moon rode in a clear sky, which boasted a few stars. I walked down the street, the main street, around 7:00 pm. There was not a soul in sight. A couple of cars drove down the street slowly. But in the distance, you could hear the cars on the highway. Like many towns, Oatlands was bypassed by the highway, so you can always hear the cars and trucks in the distance, but they never come any closer.

I walked past the antiques shop, the great jumble. A light was on inside, so you could see the space in that night-time, dim-light kind of way. I noticed, hanging from the ceiling, a tuba. The tuba is a giant instrument. I did not notice it before. Isn't it funny how you can *not* notice a tuba?

I think: the moon, the empty street, and the distant highway.
It could be the title of a poem or song.

Tuesday 29 Aug 2023

Today, I return to Hobart on the bus. It leaves this afternoon, so I have most of the day to pass. I have booked a hotel in Hobart for the next three nights. I have done my business in Oatlands; in fact, I have done my business in Tasmania for this trip. I could have made the trip shorter, but my time is always mapped out, and I wanted to relax into this more expansive notion of time. It doesn't have to be full. And much has happened in my time here, living in time without expectation.

Last night, I had the thought that if Sarah came to Oatlands straight off the *St Vincent*, having just spent more than three months heaving on the swells between England and Van Diemen's Land, she probably relived the movement of the ship when she went to sleep. This might have continued for weeks. Perhaps this was fearful; she spent much of her time on the ship in the infirmary (is that what they called it on a ship?). She had rheumatism, she vomited dark blood, and she was constipated. (There is a copy of the ship's surgeon's reports available.)

I like to think she went to Mass. It may have been her only connection with Ireland, home. I suspect that the priest, Martin McRohan, was Irish. I think that Sarah's father's first name was Martin. I haven't seen any register entries for his birth, death or marriage, but his name is in the records of her trial in London.

I packed my bag, wrote in the Guest Book, and left my "studio apartment". My only dilemma was what to do with my suitcase and backpack. The Imbibers is not open today. I decided to leave them outside my room; it was out of sight from the road. I went to the same café for morning coffee: Vintage on High. I now know that her name is Susan, and she is Ukrainian. She came out here when young. She has been in Oatlands for nearly twenty years. She bought the café and house-next-door when they were a shambles, and she has done them up, so they are very attractive.

She said the town hierarchy were intrigued by her efforts, and each week when she went to the pub for dinner as a newcomer to the town, they invited her to join them. Hierarchy means two things: it means they are wealthy, in local terms, and it means they are descendants of the original colonialists. And they kept an eye on her, as a solitary woman.

Susan also told me that she had worked at the place up the road, The Stables. It had been run by a woman who was also alone, Mrs White. Mrs White was wealthy, and she lived to be one hundred. First, Susan offered to help her to clean up the garden. It had not been looked after, and it looked poorly. So she weeded it, pulled out the dead plants, and put in new plants. She said it looked wonderful.

Next, there was a succession of casual people who took care of the kitchen in the café, and Susan ended up taking it over and turning it into a seven-day-a-week restaurant which thrived. When Mrs White died, Susan came back to her own place and started her café. Later, I had lunch at The Stables, which is now a pancake and crepes café. The attraction for me was that they offered a lemon and garlic scallops crepe, and I hadn't had a fine meal of scallops yet (the lunch I had had didn't count). It was very acceptable.

While I was in the café, a couple came in. They were both local, but the man was Australian and the woman was Irish, with a strong accent. She came from the county of Cork, from the town of Clonakilty. This is about one hundred kilometres east of Castletownbere, driving around the bays. I have friends there. Clonakilty is also close to the sea. Her special interest was black pudding. She has a friend who now makes it in Australia. I nodded politely. Apart from occasional chicken and seafood, I haven't eaten meat for over forty years.

Susan told her I was here on a quest, looking for clues about my convict ancestor. I told her that Sarah Crosby was Irish, and she had come from Waterford. It's funny in conversations, you have to judge how long the story has to be in order to fit the flow. This one had to be short, and I didn't tell the London story, how the policeman refused her entry to the refuge at night, and she lost her self-control completely, and took out a penknife and stabbed him in the arm. (Later, the newspapers described it, correctly, I imagined, as desperation.) And how two policemen manhandled her to the ground (you could say, brutally) and she was arrested. The English didn't like the Irish, although the Irish were starving because of the potato famine. And Sarah's family had disappeared (died?); she had left Ireland and come to England.

The man and Susan had lots to say. They had common friends in the town, that only saw each other occasionally, and they had lots to say about them all.

After coffee, I walked up the street again. I wanted to find the house that the Irish rebel had lived in: Kevin Izod O'Doherty. And I couldn't find it. And then I tried to find it in the photos I had taken, and I couldn't find it there either. I thought I must be mad. Had it really happened? Had I really read that story? I went slowly, and read the plaques on all the houses carefully: nothing. I thought I should step sideways from the question and have lunch, so I went to the place where I knew I could buy crepes.

After this pleasant refreshment, I realised that I had ignored one house, because workmen had been busy there replacing the roof with new corrugated iron. It was called Elm Cottage, and it was the place. Lunch had shifted my perspectives. The plaque said that Kevin O'Doherty had boarded there for some time. The house was in close proximity to the Wilmott Arms. And he would have been Catholic, so he very likely went to church on Sunday, where he might have encountered an attractive young Irish woman. I am speculating.

However, on a more careful reading of the plaque, I realised that the story was even more particular. In the 1840s, Elm Cottage was rented by John Ryan, a devout Catholic, and it was he who provided lodging for O'Doherty. Moreover, Ryan "often hosted Mass in this cottage prior to the building of St Paul's church". So, this is where Mass was held, with O'Doherty present, and in close proximity to the Wilmott Arms, where Sarah Crosby was living.

I am still speculating, but there are firm grounds for my speculation.

I walked back up the street towards the bus stop. On the way, I came to an op-shop. I had no desire to buy clothes, but they might have books, and I had sent all my books home. One should never send all of one's books home. One should keep one or two with one.

At the bookshelves I encountered another seeker. It was a man, and he was looking for a particular book by a particular author he had come to enjoy. The author had an unusual name, and he said the shops he loved the best were the ones that had organised all the fiction into alphabetical order. This was not one of those shops. However, he said the author's name was quick to identify, so it wasn't too bad. We swapped places so we could both continue our quests.

My quest was vague. I simply wanted a book to read between now and when I got home. There are lots of books that are of little interest to me, so that makes it easier. I eventually found one, which fit the bill nicely. The author, Kathryn Lomer, was Tasmanian, which seemed appropriate. The story-line crossed cultures: the protagonist went from Tasmania to Japan. And the plot involved calligraphy: brush-writing of Japanese script, which is a practice aimed at self-discipline and mastery. All in all, a book that I am likely to enjoy.

While I was purchasing that (for two dollars), I spied a book on the counter called *Oatlands*. It was thin (good) and it covered the history of Oatlands. I bought that, too. I was most pleased.

I had to cover two hours until the bus came, so I went into the Kentish Hotel where I had had lunch yesterday. They were friendly and the food was good. They had a lounge room off the side of the café. It had two large lounge chairs and a fireplace, although it was not cold enough for the fire to be lit. It looked as if it was used on cold days. I settled in there with my new reading material until it was time for the bus.

As ever, I found myself not reading on the bus. There is too much going on outside the window. The clouds to the west were intriguing, the landscape was for sheep, and it looked sparse: sheep eat right down to the ground. But the journey passed, about an hour and a half, and I arrived back in Hobart.

There was a minor incident before we got to the bus transit station (as it is called). There was a scheduled stop about five kilometres north of Hobart, and a boy of about twelve years of age was about to get off there. The bus had stopped, and the driver said to the boy, "Where's your mother?"

The boy had a mobile phone, and he said, "I think she's about ten minutes away."

The driver said, "I can't let you off the bus. You're a minor. Your mother has to be here, or I would have to wait for her to arrive." Clearly, he was not going to wait. The boy fidgeted a bit, but he wasn't fighting the driver. He was accepting of the situation as the bus driver presented it.

The driver said it again: "I'm responsible for you, and I can't leave you here without your mother. You will have to come with me to the transit station, and she will have to pick you up from there."

I watched all this. I wondered if the driver was being officious, or if there had been an incident to make them follow the rules more strictly, or if he was, in fact, being paternal. I was inclined to think there was an element of the latter. When we arrived at Hobart, the boy was introduced to the man who was on duty at the transit station, and the driver said to the boy, "He'll take care of you until your mother gets here."

So, it seemed to be accepted between the two men that they were responsible for minors until their parents arrived. Paternal? Paternalistic? I decided it was appropriate, and even comforting. Who knows what happened to the mother? Everyday issues? Chaos? Dramas? Life, as it happens?

I decided to walk from the bus stop to the hotel, despite my luggage. If one takes one's time, many things are possible, and it was all downhill. I found the hotel and checked in. I am staying three nights. It is a world apart from the Hotel Astor. This one, called Allurity, is modern. I am not sure if the name is annoying, or if I am at a stage in my journey where I am ready to be annoyed.

There was a sign on the wall in the reception area explaining that the name was made up, and they seemed proud of it. It is based on the word "allure", or "alluring". I don't like it. I wondered about this for some time. I think that liking and disliking are often unconscious. In this case, when I think or say the word, I think my mind picks up on the sound "lurid", and that would be an unattractive name, so I am sub-consciously offended.

I am also biased against made-up words if they are not necessary. Advertising and marketing are as full of them as groups of teenagers, and gangs out to make their own special code.

I made up my own word today. It just occurred to me, and I haven't heard it before, so it could be original: "crudimentary". It puts together "crude" and "rudimentary". The meanings fit together. I could argue that it adds more emphasis, but I am joking. It is, of course, appalling and unnecessary. But I could use it if I found a suitably humorous context for it. I am on the lookout.

In the meantime, I am staying at the Allurity Hotel. I am on the sixth floor. It has all the things you expect, and just a few things to annoy. All the things that annoy me are about reading and writing, so, perhaps they are not a problem to many people.

There is not a single light in the room that is sufficient for reading. And the small table on which one might write or work on a laptop, rocks: it is rickety, it is not stable. On the other hand, the room is quite adequate for watching television, which might suit most people. I, however, have resolved not to watch television while I am away. Perhaps I will not watch television when I get back home. I am observing myself, wondering if my brain is reconfiguring itself. I also note that it would be a mistake to take this too seriously.

I went out for dinner. I also wanted to see the sky. The moon should still be large, after last night's full moon. But the clouds hold sway tonight. Down a small alley I found a large Japanese restaurant, Yamashita. My choice was miso soup, followed by tempura with a selection of contents: prawns and vegetables. It was all delicious, and much appreciated.

I walked down to the wharves, because I hadn't done that since I had come back to town, and I shouldn't be stuck in my room. I watched the water and the boats for a while.

Wednesday 30 Aug 2023

It is an overcast day, grey. I fly home on Friday morning. I will go and see the antique-maps man tomorrow. I have no agenda apart from that. My mind starts to think about what people are like towards the end of their holiday. They want to buy things, as souvenirs to remind them of the holiday. They want to have discovered some great secret, and/or have enjoyed something exceptional.

The woman at the Shipwrights Arms Hotel who was very drunk, said to me that she was on holidays and she wanted to let loose, to throw off the chains of the little town she lived in. And of course, being drunk was part of that. And she was off to MONA the next day. I told her that MONA aims to be shocking. She thought that was great. I have less patience for being deliberately shocked or, perhaps, for people who are out to deliberately shock me.

It has not been necessary for me to seek out exciting things: jet skis, parachuting, fast cars and the like. That reminds me that Mrs White, the old lady wo owned The Stables in Oatlands, drove her car down to the restaurant every day for lunch. But she had her licence taken away from her when she was ninety because she was caught driving her car at one hundred and thirty kilometres an hour. Apparently, she was small but very formidable. She was quite offended that the police took her licence away.

My excitement has been in pursuing a story. I suppose it is the excitement that the detective must experience. I would not say I am obsessed, but I am definitely engaged in the story of Sarah Crosby's life, and Edward Lewis's too. The mind shuffles between logic and emotion, wondering about the facts and circumstances of their lives, and then wondering about the emotional sway of their lives.

I remember that they were all torn away from their homeland unwillingly, even if their homes were not at all stable. They were torn away from the larger surrounds of their neighbourhoods and everyone they knew. They were torn away from their countries. And the ripping away was permanent. There was no return. Moreover, the land to which they were going was crude (or crudimentary) and only roughly formed. They were not expert or eager new settlers, with ambitions. In the midst of that turmoil, did they find some serenity and direction?

The thread for me is: I have come from this. There are other threads in my family tree as well: the Cornish miners (Martin), the Scottish stonemasons (Mackie), the Oxfordshire stonemasons (Eaglestone), the Hertfordshire rural folk (Archer), to name some. These are the lives I wish to understand, and they are becoming the stories I wish to tell.

This journey has been productive. I am getting to understand Sarah's time at Oatlands a little better, piecing together another part of her life, even with the inherent uncertainty of my knowledge.

In the morning I went walking downtown, first of all, to find a coffee. There are no breakfast facilities in the hotel. This is an aspect of the hotel that is not alluring. Although, I wouldn't eat what would probably be on offer: tasteless cereals. I don't subscribe to the "I need a coffee" mentality; it's just pleasant in the mid-morning. I went back to a coffee shop near the wharves where I had been before: sometimes it's nice to go back to a place that was pleasant. Again, I avoid any suggestion that there is dependence in this. However, there is a human tension between familiarity and novelty. We like both, don't we?

I had sourdough toast and cappuccino. Let's call that breakfast. It was most enjoyable. Hobart weather has to be monitored in five-minute segments. I could have taken a photo of Mount Wellington (kunanyi) covered in low-hanging mist, and taken another photo of it five minutes later in full sun. They say this is because Tasmania is a small island, and the winds from the sea blow in all the time, ever-changing.

I walked down the wharves to the end, where the old IXL warehouses are. I wondered about the origin of the IXL name, and the plaques offer an explanation. (Tasmania is easy in this respect.)

Henry Jones built up his business empire from nothing. He started out on the factory floor. The name IXL means "I excel (at everything I do)". I think this is a commendable sentiment. However, he was also hard on his employees, and mean with his wages.

The plaque mentions that there was a Royal Commission in 1907, and he was heavily criticised for his treatment of employees. What the plaque doesn't say is that 1907 was the year of the Harvester decision in the High Court, a decision which set Australia on a path towards minimum wages for all workers. I learned that when I did employment law in my Bachelor of Business degree at Southern Cross University, finished in 1997 (when I was forty-seven).

There were several plaques in the vicinity: there is a lot of history in this corner of the wharves. There is no island nearby now, because the area between it and the shore was filled in. It was initially called Hunter Island, and it was where the first expedition landed in 1804. At that time, you could walk across at low tide, but not at high tide. The island was useful because it was secure, so it meant food and provisions could not be stolen. Over the years, the convicts filled in the space to the mainland with rocks, all by hand. They say it took 5,000 cubic metres.

When Henry Jones' jam factory developed, the area became a squalid neighbourhood of workers' homes. The 1920s were when the jam business was at its peak, because Henry Jones had gone to England and arranged for the export of jam to England. There was a burgeoning gentry class in Hobart. In the 1890s there was a devastating fire among the houses; most of them were destroyed. There were fire brigades, but they could not get into the narrow laneways to fight the fire.

There is much that gets forgotten. Occasionally some of it is rediscovered. In the 1980s, when workmen were digging up the roadway there in order to make improvements, they dug up a great deal of ash, remnants of that fire.

I decided to go back to the museum, because my trip there had been in the afternoon, and it was possible that I missed things.

Indeed, I did; I missed a whole floor, and an entire building. The floor was upstairs in the main building, and it contained artworks. I took notice of a large painting (about two metres wide) which was of Hobart in 1854. It was what Hobart would have looked like when Sarah and Edward were there.

I took a photograph, although that is only a rough idea of the painting. The vantage point of the picture was out on the water looking in at the wharves and the township. At this point in time it was a well-settled township., and busy. Did Sarah and Edward think of staying and living their lives here? I suspect that they did not want to, because ex-convicts were looked down upon. Sarah had been given an order that her Ticket of Leave was on the condition that she did not reside in Hobart; although, I suspect that that order was not enforced very rigidly. Edward and Sarah stayed in Hobart for two to three years after she received her ticket of leave.

Another item that attracted my attention was some woodwork. It was a hall-seat, some carved wooden panels, and a mantelpiece. It was all very nice. The explanation said that they were carved by Hobart women in 1907. That was a revelation! There was a group of women (well-off and looking for something to do) who took up wood-carving. Some of their work was displayed overseas.

The inspiration for them was the Arts and Crafts movement that was lively in America around the turn of the century (1900). Theirs was a reaction against the industrialised world, and they designed houses, furniture, furnishings, ornaments, and gardens. Their work is beautiful, not "modern" or "modernist". I reveal my biases. I have a book from the American arts and crafts movement that was first published in 1909. It is a facsimile edition published in 1979. It is called *Craftsman Homes*, by Gustav Stickley. I still love the houses and the furniture and furnishings.

I remember that I bought Stickley's book when I was renovating my house in Horseshoe Creek, near Kyogle. I won't say that much of the book translated into my renovations, but the spirit was there.

There were several groups of children at the museum. Some of them were in the building that I had missed the other day, the natural history museum. There were many stuffed animals and birds, including some which are rare. Tasmanians killed many animals and birds in the colonial days. They interfered with their English sensibilities and their bid to develop an English countryside.

One exhibit was of the skulls of about thirty eagles. One story was about the discovery that platypuses lay eggs. This was a fact of wonderment! Prince Albert (one of Queen Victoria's sons) came to Hobart in 1868. He was the first royalty to visit the Australian colonies, and he was very popular. One of my great great grandfathers, William Archer, started a hotel at Pyrmont in Sydney around 1880. It was called the Duke of Edinburgh, which was the prince's title. In fact, there was a spate of hotels around Australia called the Duke of Edinburgh around this time.

I had a modest lunch at the museum café. Afterwards, I thought I would walk back to the hotel. But I realised I was close to Fullers' Bookshop, and I hadn't been in there yet. What could there be in this southern outpost of a bookshop? More than one person I had talked to had mentioned Fuller's as being a place I should visit.

There were some lovely books there, some with interesting perspectives on life. And odd things. I had read a story in the last couple of years about an Australian woman who had gone on a pilgrimage across Spain (*Sinning across Spain*, by Alisa Piper), but there was a book here about a woman who had dragged a forty-kilogram stone to Norway from England, to be placed at a cathedral. She had completed a stonemason's training course in England. That was an interesting endeavour.

There was a book in the Philosophy section on the topic of "distraction" (*The Wandering Mind,* by Jamie Kreiner). The author examined medieval monks and their engagement with the issue. I think the author of the book on the forty-kilogram stone might have understood it. The author of the book on distraction started by talking about modern life and mobile phones, but she was making the point that distraction has been an issue for a long time.

I agree, to a point, but as Peter Senge pointed out in *The Fifth Discipline*, there are two modes of thought, and you have to be able to do both, and know when each is appropriate. They are convergent and divergent thinking. Sometimes you have to narrow in and concentrate (convergent), but at other times you have to defocus, and allow your thinking to widen out, in order to pick up new perspectives and ideas (divergent). Am I going to buy and read the book? No; my list is already growing, and if I give in too often, then, by the time I get to a new book, I wonder why I was interested in it in the first place.

But, walking into a bookshop does refresh one's thinking.

Another book I was attracted to was *The Failures of Philosophy* (by Stephen Gaukroger). I thought this might explain why I have always been wary of philosophy, and would not call myself a philosopher, and yet I recognise that many people would be tempted to call me a philosopher. I didn't buy it, but I am still interested in it. I liked his table of contents. I fear, however, that he writes too philosophically for me. I need a break from the abstract nouns. I want to understand, but I find myself drowning in the words.

I did find several books that I own; this has become part of my interest now. But that is another example of the tension between familiarity and novelty. It's nice to see that I've read books that are commonly on offer these days, but I also like to find books that no one has heard about; something that would be called obscure. We are made up of tensions, and it is our task to find the appropriate balance between them. Or, I suppose, we could call them contradictions. I prefer to see them as tensions.

That is why I am wary of the book on distractions: what is it we are being distracted from? It may be best not to have too rigid a distinction between what is deemed to be a valid object of attention, and what is a distraction. We are a river; we flow. And sometimes, our very safety depends on our paying attention to our environment, taking the wide view. I think of the infinity symbol I traced in the air when I was talking with the priest. Our equanimity is a balanced movement between this end and the other end.

I left the bookshop without buying a single book. It is possible, although I generally like to buy something. It's like going into a church and putting a penny in the plate.

I have realised that I am very close to the State Library. I did not plan that.

I have seen no tubas today.

I went out again around 6:30 pm, in search of dinner before all the cafes and restaurants close. Walking down the street, I saw the moon. It was between the buildings and it looked big and round. To my eyes, it could have been full. Satisfied with that, I continued, in search of a Thai restaurant. I thought I remembered where there was one, near a bus stop.

There was no one dining in it when I arrived, but it was peak hour, and people came in to buy take-away. My meal was adequate. It was a cold night; I even heard a passerby tell her friend it was a cold night, so I must have been right. Rather than walking around, I decided to go straight back to the hotel.

Even at night, the seagulls fly up around the buildings, squawking in the city lights. The seagulls let you know you are close to the sea.

I have not seen television for almost two weeks, since I left home. What does it mean? Was it just a bad habit? Was it a pathetic addiction? Was it lazy to sit and watch television at night? Or am I being too harsh on myself? Why am I not watching television?

Earlier, I talked about the book, *Distraction*. Television, like all technologies that involve screens, are the opposite: they capture attention. Not for any good purpose, but just because. The only screens in our society that do not do this are parking meter screens; most of them are virtually unreadable – you cannot read any words or numbers on the tiny screens, or the instructions, in the available light, amid the reflections that are bouncing off the screen. Sometimes, in addition, their logic is not self-evident.

But, television screens are boldly lit and richly coloured, and the images are moving. They capture attention. The process is reversed. When you pick up a book, it is generally because you are interested in the story or the topic, the way I was in the bookshop, picking up books. But you watch the television first, to see what is showing. It takes effort to resist that pull.

What happens when you eliminate that? I still have to watch screens: my mobile phone and my laptop, to check messages and to skim the news. I still stay in touch; I might discover, one morning, that the world has been destroyed and I can't (or don't need to) go out there anymore. Or my plane to fly home is on strike. But the reality is, this is not greatly time-consuming, not like it could be.

I think that watching television just filled my head up with inconsequential thoughts. If that is the case, it turns out that it was all a distraction! The big question, however, is: a distraction from what? One could say I am taking this too seriously, but my response is: and what if I'm not?

However, the deeper question is, how much of this society do I forgo? My warning to society is this: there is a great deal that I don't need from you. I don't need new clothes constantly; there are many new artefacts that I have no need for (or desire); I don't need a great deal of entertainment. And yet, I use electricity, cars, trains, food suppliers, a variety of institutions, and yes, occasionally I am a consumer of movies and music.

It seems that, in seeking to live sanely and modestly, one comes up against the whole phalanx of modern society. There seems to be an undertow of loyalty tugging at you, as if you owe it to society to appropriate as much of what it offers as you can. It's as if decent new shoes will not be available to me when I need them (which may only be once every five years) unless I purchase new shoes much more regularly, otherwise the suppliers will go out of business. And anyway, new shoes are so much cheaper now than they used to be, because of global commerce and mass-manufacturing.

At street-level, that is, in the conversation of ordinary people, these are the kinds of arguments that float around. Mostly they are not articulated, and mostly the logic is sloppy, but there they are. Supposedly, in a society where people have freedom, things will find their own eventual balance that is a balance between supply and demand. At this point, everyone will survive and be happy.

My caution is that I think you have to establish a personal lifestyle that is satisfactory before you start planning the whole world for everyone. Even if you can't see how everything would work if it worked the way it would suit you. In the end, it's a simple goal: get it right for yourself first, as long as you are not harming others or devastating the world. Be happy, create harmony.

Think of the years gone by, when most people consumed very little, and yet their lives were still worth living.

Thursday 31 Aug 2023

Today: my last day in Hobart. I am returning home to Sydney tomorrow morning. Later today, I will go to the antique-maps guy and see if he has a copy of the map I want. In the meantime, I could go to the library. My reason? It is close, and they have a nice café there.

The library café is light, airy and friendly. I had lemon poppyseed cake and coffee. I noticed also that they had a selection of teas available, including Russian Caravan. I applaud their taste.

August is Family History Month, so today is the last day. I should honour that by going to the library and doing some research. I decided to spend a little time looking up Charles Sutton. I have learned that he was a convict, but when was he transported, and what was he transported for?

In the Tasmanian Names Index I did find some details, although not everything. He got married in 1827 to Sarah Wright, who was two years younger than him, at Hobart. Charles could not read or write (his signature was denoted by an X ("his mark"), but Sarah could read and write: she signed her name). It was amusing that he should marry a woman called Wright, because he was a wheelwright.

I confirmed that he had been a convict. He had been tried in Middlesex in 1817, and transported for seven years. The ship was the *Dromedary*. However, the record did not say what he had been convicted for. There was another record that said he (my Charles Sutton?) was charged with sheep-stealing. It was an impressive feat: ninety-five sheep and fifteen lambs. But, the charge was in 1829, and in any case, the person was found Not Guilty. One would want to know more details about that case. Why was the person found not guilty, or, alternatively, why was he ever charged?

He had allegedly stolen the sheep from George Green, and the trial was in the Supreme Court, but the records didn't say where the trial was; it could have been in Oatlands (they had a Supreme Court) or Hobart.

Charles Sutton (my Charles Sutton) purchased various parcels of land, first at Ross, then at Oatlands. Perhaps this included the land on which the inn was established.

I will have to dig back into my information when I get home. At least I have the general picture of Charles's life. And I also know that when Charles died, Sarah Sutton took over the running of the inn, then assumed its licence.

Addendum

(From research back at home): Sarah Sutton got married again, to John Newby, a year after Charles died. They were both "Innkeepers". She outlived him as well. He died in 1876. She died in 1888.

I have discovered numerous women, on this trip, who took life into their own hands, like the women at the Museum who took up wood-carving and achieved a high level of skill and the praise of the public back in 1907.

Sarah Sutton was not to be stopped by the death of her husband. She had been by Charles's side for over twenty years. She was the one who could read and write. It seems that she was well capable of managing her own affairs.

After I arrived home, I got back into searching for the reasons for Charles Sutton's transportation. In the records of the Old Bailey, his trial is found in 1819 on a charge of burglary, along with two other young men.

A new scenario for Sarah Crosby springs to mind; Charles and Sarah Sutton's son, also called Charles, who was born in 1831, was the one who had a tryst with her. The young Charles was about the same age as her. And could Charles Sutton's wife have been the one who found out about the incident, and had Sarah Crosby sent back to Hobart, to Cascades Female Factory? This is a plausible scenario too. I can think of various motivations for all of the parties.

I also accept that it is possible that Charles Sutton, the father, was the one in Sarah Crosby's bed. It was not uncommon in the convict days for the employer of female convicts (who were mostly domestic servants) to engage in sex with them; if the employer wished to do this, the convict had little choice in the matter. One author has pointed out that male convicts generally worked outside, on roads, fences, timber-getting, and tending animals, while women convicts generally worked indoors, so they were always around their employers. There was more opportunity for sexual incidents to occur.

From a position of having no idea who the man in Sarah's bed might be, I now have three or four possibilities: Charles Sutton, her employer, husband of Sarah Sutton, and father of Charles Sutton, or Charles Sutton the son, or the Irish rebel, Kevin Izod O'Doherty, or, someone else. I also wonder about the formulation of the charge, "she was found with a man in her bed", because I can't imagine her sleeping quarters were, as they say, salubrious, or private, and it seems just as likely that such an event occurred in the male's lodgings.

The wording infers that Sarah Crosby orchestrated the event, whereas it seems unlikely that that was true. The abiding thought, in all this, is that it is likely that Sarah Sutton played an active role in the outcome. She strikes me as being a person of some power. Perhaps she was the one who wanted to get Sarah Crosby out of the way, which would be true whether it was her husband, her son or the Irishman who was the culprit.

Now that I have new things to think about, I will go for a walk. Perhaps I will meander down to the shop of the Antique Maps guy. I did, but I discovered his door closed. He could be here; he could be upstairs, but I could also go and have some lunch. I found a shop along the wharves and had lunch. It was salmon sushi; the salmon was good.

Although I have been through Salamanca before, I know there are some galleries I have not been to yet, so I return. I go up a set of stairs, and I see that there is a gallery called the Sidebar Gallery, because it is along a landing from the main part of the building. I brave the unusual route and find myself in a room that features one artist. Her paintings are black brush paintings, like Chinese or Japanese calligraphy. The exhibition is called "Ink in Motion".

The artist is present; her name is eastern European: Margaret Skowronski (it is actually Polish). She has travelled to both Japan and China. I love the paintings, but I don't understand the connections. How does it happen that someone who originates in eastern Europe comes to be living in Hobart and painting brushwork in Chinese or Japanese fashion? I suppose it is no less unusual than a Ukrainian woman living in Oatlands and running a café.

It is salient that Margaret Skowronski's paintings appear now, because the book I bought in Oatlands was called *The God in the Ink*, and it is about a woman who went from Tasmania to Japan and who learned to paint Zen-style with brush and ink. Margaret's workshop is Blackmans Bay Studio.

After I had looked around, I said I liked her work, and I asked her (best to be straightforward): how does it happen that you come from eastern Europe, you live in Tasmania, and you make these paintings of Chinese or Japanese brushwork? There was no special reason, except that she liked it, and thought that it was evocative. Saying that she was drawn to it would be classed as a bad pun, but perhaps there is something in the metaphor.

Margaret said that she wanted viewers to put their own interpretation on the paintings: "What do you see in it?" To emphasise this point, the title of some of the paintings was "Untitled". She pointed to one, and asked me what came to mind. I felt that it was dancing: someone standing and dancing, their legs swirling around, their arms spread out in the wind. She said that many other people see dancing in this painting too.

I had a question for her, as well: had she heard of the I Ching? To my surprise, she had not. I told her that I consult the I Ching regularly, and the ideographs for the sixty-four hexagrams evoke similar impressions to her paintings. The I Ching is thousands of years old. Fortunately, when I am travelling, I have Alfred Huang's version of the I Ching on my phone, so I was able to show her the cover, and one of the hexagrams. She was intrigued. There were obvious resonances between the two worlds.

Her paintings were for sale, but I was not buying: I am travelling. However, she had some cards printed, and I bought several of those. It was a mutually interesting encounter.

When I entered, she was reading. The book? *Breakfast with Seneca: A Stoic Guide to the Art of Living*, by David Fideler. She recommended it to me; she said it seemed like a wise philosophy of life. She said she had bought it when she went to Fuller's Bookshop to ask them to put up a poster for her exhibition.

I walked down to a lower level in the building, and there was another exhibition. It consisted of impressionistic landscapes. The artist, Hannah Blackmore, called them "contemplative landscape paintings". They had soft edges, moody colours and shimmering depths. I looked around, and enjoyed her work.

I saw her walking back into an office, and I commented that her brochure indicated that the exhibition was due to start tomorrow. That was true. She had just finished setting up, and the opening was tonight. She had that buoyancy people have when they have just finished a momentous task. She assured me that it was okay for people to view the paintings now. There was another person in the gallery too. I wished her well.

I walked back to the maps shop. The door was closed, but I pressed the buzzer. He was inside, and he came to open the door. He remembered me, and my request. First, he had to wonder where the copy was, but I was confident it would soon appear, and it did. He showed it to me, rolling it out on a table. He had made another copy for himself as well. He said he could have treated it as an antique print, by sponging it first to make it damp, then sprinkling some tea

102

over it until it picked up the stain and looked aged. He was suggesting that I might like that.

I said thanks, but my purpose was for family history research, and plain was appropriate. He understood. I told him that I had realised that the map also contained the street where Edward and Sarah lived after they got married, and where their twins were born: Watchorn Street. He said he thought Watchorn had been the Mayor at one time, or was a dignitary in the early colony.

Later, I looked up Watchorn. Gerard had been correct, on both counts, but the truth was more nuanced. Yes, John Watchorn had been the Mayor of Hobart, but that was not until 1890, and again from 1894 to 1896, so that was not why the street had received its name. He had migrated from Nottingham to Van Diemen's Land in 1837 with his family as a boy of eleven. Given the dates, I suspect that the street was named after his father. John became a publican and wine merchant; perhaps he acquired that business from his father.

Gerard realised he should dig out the details of the map he had copied for me. It had come from a particular book. The map was printed by Mr Robin Hood (yes, we both laughed about that), who had a print shop near to where we are now. I told him that in my family tree I had a family called Hood, but they came from Scotland, not Nottingham, where the legendary Robin Hood resided. He showed me a short biography of the printer, Robin (Vaughan) Hood, and I copied that.

Finally, he found a postage tube so I could store the map safely in that, and he rolled it up for me. Job done. At the last minute, he included one of his prints in the tube. It was a print of a Tasmanian tiger, "Thylacinus cynocephalus".

Addendum

When I got home, I looked up the print of the Tasmanian tiger. The picture that Gerard gave me comes from a book by John Gould published in 1863: *The Mammals of Australia*. Note, the thylacine is actually a meat-eating marsupial, and the name "tiger" is not accurate; the scientific name means "pouched dog with a wolf head". The print carried the name H.C. Richter. He had drawn them from real life, in England. A pair of thylacines was sent to England and it arrived at Regents Park Zoo in London in 1850.

There is even a connection to Louisa Anne Meredith in this thylacine picture. She traced Gould's picture in order to include thylacines in her book *Tasmanian Friends and Foes*. And then I start to wonder where I have seen this picture before, noting that I haven't seen either Meredith's book or Gould's book. It is this image that is used on the label of Cascade Premium Lager beer. Of course! (Although, it should also be said that this picture is the most common one of the thylacine that is reproduced, according to an article by the University of Tasmania, who held an exhibition on the thylacine in 2007.)

A friend of mine later told me that he had bought a print of a Tasmanian Aborigine about thirty years ago in Hobart, and we worked out that it was the same shop, and the same man from whom he had bought it. He had the same manner towards people. I felt that in the street map, I had found something that was quite rare, and quite relevant to my inquiries, and he was a most interesting man. It was a very satisfying encounter.

The afternoon was cooling. A cold wind was blowing through the town. The next morning, I was waiting for the bus to the airport, and two other ladies were waiting as well. They said they had heard that it snowed yesterday afternoon, up on kunanyi.

On the way back to the hotel, I looked for some food for dinner. Tonight, I was going to try doing yoga on Zoom, and I wanted some food for after that, so it couldn't be hot food; I didn't have a microwave to heat up food. I decided on sushi. There were two or three shops to pick from.

I managed to do yoga satisfactorily. The class uses props, and I didn't have any props with me (blocks, cushions, a chair etc), but it would be interesting to see how I could make do without them. And it was fine, and interesting; not ideal, but fine.

After the yoga class I was looking out the window, because it is not often I am up on the sixth floor. And I realised that one of the things that is different between Hobart and where I live in Sydney is that you never hear planes in Hobart. They come into Tasmania over the east coast, and the airport is east of the city, and the planes leave the same way. So, they don't fly over the city.

Where I live in Sydney – the northwest – the planes fly over, even though they are still a fair way up and the sound is not too intrusive. In Hobart, the only aircraft I have heard is a helicopter.

Friday 1 Sep 2023

My flight leaves early: 9:45 am. I always make sure I have plenty of time, so it is useless my thinking about doing anything other than getting ready for the flight. I packed successfully, made time for a cup of green tea, and was twenty minutes early for the airport bus. Two ladies waited as well. One of them had a handbag with the word "Amsterdam" plastered all over it. I thought it was good that she wouldn't be booking it in, because it could end up on the other side of the world.

It was a chilly morning. No snow in town, true, but it was chilly. Nevertheless, some passersby, whom I would presume are locals, were in shirtsleeves. It may have been ritualistic: it is the first day of spring.

Approaching the check-in desk at the airport, I experience trepidation. What is the correct procedure? I had checked in on my laptop back at the hotel, but if I was in Sydney, I would have had to print the luggage tag out before approaching the desk. Here, there did not seem to be any machines to do that. But, boldly, I lined up and approached the desk. It was all cheery. It seemed that I had committed no errors.

I could demand a printed sign to assist me, but I am exhausted with signs. One idea I have for writing a book is to spend a day writing down or recording every sign I encountered in going around the city. That would be the book. So, for example, the repeated announcement about not leaving your luggage unattended would get recorded. In fact, it would get recorded every time you heard it while you were sitting there waiting.

If you were on a train, and the announcement gave the name of every station at which the train was going to stop, that would be recorded. Would there be inherent poetry in such a book? Or would it be the most infuriating book ever written? Would it be popular, or even wildly popular? Would a plot emerge out of this foray into the city? And would there be a sequel? Would it be revealed that the machine-voices have been talking to each other all along?

I lined up for the security inspection, and was singled out for an inspection for explosives. The task is carried out with due deference. There is no intent on the part of the officer to personally offend the traveller, and we all cooperate because we jointly value our safety, or is it our shared ideal of safety?

Whilst this charade was being performed, I remembered that a long time ago, when I lived in the country near Kyogle, I had written a short story about a man who described himself as an unexploded bomb. This was long before the nine-eleven episode in New York in 2001, or the advent of suicide bombers. At the time, I was intrigued by the idea of people who die unexpectedly at a relatively young age. They just seemed to check out of here without warning.

I thought that the singer, Nicolette Larson, was in this category. I thought she had had a brain aneurism, unexpectedly, at forty-five. (Later, I discovered that the truth was more complicated, and prescription drugs were involved.) Eva Cassidy was another one; she was thirty-three. I thought that she had had a brain aneurism too. However, I later discovered that she had had cancer.

In the story, I suggested that we are all unexploded bombs: that any one of us could just go at some point. I was not being fatalistic. I was just saying we don't know what is going to happen in our lives, and we might live more positively if we recognised this. Then, if we died today, it might be seen that we had appreciated life. I smiled while the explosives inspection was underway. I didn't attempt to explain why.

I bought a coffee and a muffin and enjoyed them in my alien surroundings. I also read some of my novel. Fortunately, after a long-enough pause, there was an announcement that the plane was about to board. In the meantime, my son sent me an image from home: my parcel had arrived. It had just beaten me home.

The plane was full. The journey was uneventful. We arrived in Sydney early. Emotionally, this is a strange time. I have been setting out on adventures each day, even though they were modest adventures. Now, it is over. How do I feel? Satisfied, disappointed? Did something not happen that I had hoped would happen? I think back to other journeys I have taken over the years, and how my feelings have changed. I think that now I have more equanimity. I am not so much a roller coaster.

At the same time, this makes it more difficult to talk about one's time away, because most people want to hear about excitement. Moreover, if it was not what they consider to be exciting, they are disappointed: not me, but them!

However, many of my satisfactions are not what people call exciting. One very satisfying aspect of my visit to Tasmania in winter is that I handled the cold very well. The last few years I have been thinking that my body likes the winter cold less and less as I get older. This winter, I decided that I should not think that way. I should trust my body to be resilient, and that I don't need to shrink into a corner cringing until summer comes.

It is not a matter of saying "this works", as if it were a technique, but of having a robust state of mind. The presence of people in shirt-sleeves in Hobart is enough evidence of the importance of a state of mind. I didn't see those people cringing, shivering, or covered in goose-pimples. I have been sensible, but I have not shrunk from activities because the weather was cold.

I have a warm coat that keeps out the wind; that's important. I keep my feet warm. But I have done things I thought I would avoid. It is a balance of mental strength and physical preparation.

When I think about food, again I am satisfied. There were three things I wanted to experience: a good meal of salmon, a good meal of scallops, and a good platter of Tasmanian cheeses. I didn't know how these were going to happen, but they all did. I started with a scallops meal down on the wharves, and it was disappointing. I could qualify that by saying it was satisfactory but not memorable. The scallops were not big and soft and tasty, but small: scrawny and parsimonious to taste. The salmon meal did happen down on the wharves, at a fish-and-ship shop; and the fish tasted beautiful.

The cheese platter happened at Oatlands, at The Imbibers. They prepared for me a beautiful selection of cheeses, and they were all Tasmanian. Lastly, the scallops, upon which I had given up hope, also happened at Oatlands, at The Stable, with the scallops crepe.

I don't claim to be a food connoisseur. And there are many things I do not like, so I am probably banned from ever joining the ranks of connoisseurs, but there are a few things I do like, and I managed to experience them on my trip.

When I came home, I was near the end of Kathryn Lomer's book. The next morning, after putting my clothes in the washing machine, I sat down in the sun and finished reading the book. There is a paragraph near the end where the author revisits her home town in Tasmania, and it is experiencing a makeover from rural locality to tourist destination. She remarks on the irony of the town's new look being the old look, with the verandahs that jut out over the footpath down the main street.

The town is being scrubbed and polished, painted and offered up to tourists. "It is as if the present is too daunting, or incomprehensible, or too open-ended." I guess you could argue that about Oatlands, but that is not my point. My point would relate to the study of family history: it is as if the present is too daunting…. But that is not the all of it. It is also true that it is enjoyable to be on a quest.

The past is interesting because it is how we got here. The priest I spoke to at Oatlands had been an army chaplain, and he had taught recruits at a military college. The recruits were told that the most important subject they would study was history, because it is how we got here. The present is a product of what has happened. Just so, I have been trying to understand how Sarah Crosby got from one place to another in her life.

I learned from the book that in sumi-e, or ink painting, there is a concept called "in-en". The painter picks up the brush; that is "in": the painter decides. If the painter does not decide, and take action, nothing happens. The painter must set things in motion. That is the beginning. But, once things are in motion, there is "en". Flow takes over. Things happen as they will, not necessarily how the painter wants them to be. It is the interplay between control and allowing that gives rise to the painting. It is entering into this interplay that enables the painting to express spirit, rather than being a flat imitation of something in life.

And the interplay plays out. One must always be ready to begin again. "If you lose the will to begin, you lose the will to live." Do not be afraid to begin again.

This is not too serious for my search for clues about the lives of Sarah Crosby and Edward Lewis. I begin a new trail, and I look for clues. On this trip, I have looked for Sarah at Oatlands in 1850, and new possibilities have arisen. New perspectives, too. She was a girl of about thirteen when she left her home in Waterford, or rather, when she fled for her life in the midst of the potato famine. By the time she got to Oatlands, she was on the verge of womanhood, without family to protect her, or parents to guide her.

The new perspectives hover, taking shape, to be fitted into the larger jigsaw of her life. After little more than three months, she was banished from the inn at Oatlands and sent to Cascades Female Factory in Hobart. Her future lay elsewhere. But I think that Sarah had the determination to start again, every time. She did not shrink, except when she was sick and needed to lie low to recover. She gave birth to eight children in all, and lived to be sixty-four. I like to think she had "in-en".

I still have threads to follow. That is the way of it when you venture out into the wild. I have maps, notes, pictures, passages from the historical plaques to process and digest. It needs tidying up and making sense of. And it was a winter trip. I didn't venture into really cold places. But I have come home and it has turned into spring. I will spend time at my tasks and bring things to fruition. Perhaps there will be further revelations as I work my way through my material.

This trip was well-paced: not hectic, and not idle. There was time enough for jazz, boat trips, bus trips, and conversations. There was scope enough for discoveries: marvellous caves, and enjoyment of academic recognition: my Diploma of Family History. There was reconnection with familiar places: the Hotel Astor, the Hobart waterfront, and Mount Wellington (kunanyi) in all its moods. There were surprises, especially Cascades Female Factory in its new glory.

A couple of days after I came home, I went shopping to replenish the cupboard. It happened to be Father's Day, so everyone was there having morning tea for their favourite father. The car park was crowded. I drove to the end section, because most people don't like to drive that far, but it was also very busy. I am always thinking, if it is too crowded, I will simply go home and come back later. So, there is no sense of urgency or panic.

I came right to the end of the car park, and there was no spot for me yet. In front of me was a large four-wheel drive, stopped. Why was it stopped? At the car in front of it, an old couple had started to load their groceries into the boot of their car. The big car had decided to wait for them, blocking the traffic, no matter how long it took. To make the situation even more amusing, the old couple had not put their groceries into shopping bags; it was all loose, and they were transferring them one item at a time.

The big car was still going to wait it out. I didn't honk the horn, but my window was open, and I waved my arm to suggest that it would be best if he moved on. There is a belief underlying this behaviour. The belief is that this is the last car spot in the park, and they don't want to miss out on it. If the driver had gone to the carpark's exit, he would see that there was a constant flow of cars. It would be okay.

Eventually, the big car reluctantly decided to move on. While all this was happening, two car spaces further on, another car had left, and the big car slid into that spot with relief. The funny thing is that, three car spaces further up, there was another spot, and it had been there the whole time. I slid into that spot, smiling. I had just come from a city of a quarter of a million people back into a city of four million. Yet, it is the same life that continues.

111

Since coming home, I have talked to a few different people. They have asked me about my trip. It makes me wonder what governs my answers. What do I choose to tell each person? How much do I tell them? It seems that we are always making those judgements, but I have never heard this discussed. What do I tell each person?

Sometimes, the governing factor is time. You can see that the appropriate answer must fit into a thirty-second time frame, and must be of a certain emotional orientation. For example, I went to Hastings Caves. I had never heard of them, but they are fantastic. There are so many stairs, up and down, and the stalactites and stalagmites are amazing.

Or, I went to my graduation. It was fine. Universities are good at doing ceremony. There was a brass quartet that played classical pieces, and the national anthem, but also, the tune to my high school's anthem. The Chancellor didn't shake anyone's hand. There were about two hundred graduating students. I think shaking hands is a casualty of COVID.

Sometimes, the person will prompt you with questions. Some people knew I was chasing family history, and I told the story of how I had met a priest at the Roman Catholic church at Oatlands. The question was, did he give you any new information? And the answer was "Yes!" He told me that if a church was being built during the time that Sarah was in Oatlands, then Mass would most certainly have been held on Sundays, somewhere near the site. I would not have found this out any other way.

When there was more time, I talked about the priest describing himself as a hermit, and what this seemed to mean.

I talked about the Mawson's Hut Replica Museum, and how humans resolve to adventure into forbidding places, just to defy the extremes. I described how one man and his entire sled team – with all the dogs – disappeared into a crevasse: death in an instant. I talked about the library that was in the hut, and how the guide knew

112

so much about it and talked for five minutes non-stop. And how gratified I was about that.

The idea of keeping a diary on my travels is well-established for me; I have written such diaries many times. It began when I was a Boy Scout and I went on hikes over the weekend and kept a log. It was theoretically part of Boy Scout culture, but most boys did not take it seriously. I did. I wrote a diary when I visited Tasmania for the first time, in December 1973. I don't keep a diary all the time; only when I am travelling. I kept one when I went to Asia in 2006, and in 2018 when I went to England and Ireland.

However, on this trip to Tasmania, what began as a diary grew into something more, something that could be a book, albeit slim. I recently discovered *Boswell's London Journal, 1762-1763* when I was sorting through books in my library. One part of that story is how it was known that he had written a huge number of letters, manuscripts and journals, but after his death, and the years passed, it was thought that most of them had been destroyed. This was not the case, and in the early twentieth century, different caches of these documents came to light and were successively published. That is one story.

The other story is about the documents themselves. *Boswell's London Journal* is the fruit of an intention by James Boswell to record his life. His journals "served the purpose, vital to him, of a mirror in which he could capture and observe his own behaviour. 'I should live no more than I can record,' he once wrote, 'as one should not have more corn growing than one can get in.' His inexhaustible interest in James Boswell, which fluctuated between extravagant self-esteem and equally extravagant self-deprecation, kept his pen busy." (p. ix, Publisher's Note, *Boswell's London Journal, 1762-1763,* The Reprint Society, London, 1952)

The story of Boswell's journals has been loosely known to me since I was a young man, but only with this recent encounter with the book in my library has my interest been sparked in Boswell's idea of writing one's life. It is much easier to contemplate this in smaller chunks, such as a trip for ten days, especially when the trip will concern matters that I wish to record and ponder.

Boswell's greater goal, of recording everything about his life that he is capable of examining and considering, is more ambitious. These days, in the wake of James Joyce's *Ulysses*, with its exhaustive coverage of twenty-four hours in a man's life, and our knowledge of the unimaginable depths and layers of our consciousness, it seems like an unfathomable goal.

Yet, it should also be noted that Boswell had been encouraged to think of himself as a writer, so writing a diary or journal was not an alien pursuit; for him, it was part and parcel of living. Similarly, it is not an alien pursuit for me to write. It is an easy occupation of my time. And my purpose is not dissimilar: to write in order to observe, remember, understand, and see resonances between moments and situations.

It may be that my journal lacks in plot. Perhaps it lacks in everything: characterisation, description of settings, analysis of situations. However, it may offer the freshness of first impressions, my recurrent encounters with surprise, and my efforts to follow the thread of living, and to "get in" the corn I have sowed.

I am reminded of a song by Paul Simon, called "Rewrite". In it, a man is always working on the rewrite of his novel. He says, "I'll eliminate the pages where the father has a breakdown and he has to leave the family, but he really meant no harm." What then? "I'm gonna substitute a car chase and a race across the rooftops, when the father saves the children and he holds them in his arms". (from the album "So Beautiful or So What?", 2011)

I apologise for the lack of car chases.

Books mentioned

Ralph K. Andrist, 1962, *Heroes of Polar Exploration*, Cassell-Caravel, New York.

James Boswell, *Boswell's London Journal, 1762-1763*, first published 1950 by The Reprint Society, London.

Becky Chambers, 2021, *A Psalm for the Wild-Built: Monk and Robot*, ebook, Tor Publishing Group.

Charles Dickens, 1839, *Oliver Twist*.

Charles Dickens, 1861, *Great Expectations*.

David Fideler, 2023, *Breakfast with Seneca: A Stoic Guide to the Art of Living*, Norton.

Stephen Gaukroger, 2023, *The Failures of Philosophy*, Princeton University Press.

John Gould, 1863, *The Mammals of Australia*.

Annie Grace, 2020, *The Alcohol Experiment,* Avery, New York.

Gunter Grass, 1959, *The Tin Drum*.

Steve Harris, 2019, *The Lost Boys of Mr Dickens*, Melbourne Books.

Alanna Hill, 2018, *Butterfly on a Pin: A Memoir of Love, Despair and Reinvention,* Hardie Grant.

David Jensen, no date, *Hobart's Antarctic History*, Mawson's Hut Foundation.

Jamie Kreiner, 2023, *The Wandering Mind*, Norton.

Kathryn Lomer, 2001, *The God in the Ink*, University of Queensland Press.

Louisa Anne Meredith, 1852, *My Home in Tasmania*.

Louisa Anne Meredith, 1860, *Some of My Bush Friends in Tasmania*.

Louisa Anne Meredith, 1880, *Tasmanian Friends and Foes, Feathered, Furred and Finned*.

Michael Nash, 2020, *Convict Places: A Guide to Tasmanian Sites*, Navarine Publishing, Hobart.

Ailsa Piper, 2012, *Sinning across Spain*, Victory Books.

Walter B. Pridmore, 2010, *Oatlands: A Colonial Treasure*.

Henry Handel Richardson, 1917, *The Fortunes of Richard Mahony: Australia Felix*, William Heinemann; 1971, Penguin.

Henry Handel Richardson, 1925, *The Fortunes of Richard Mahony: The Way Home*, William Heinemann; 1971, Penguin.

Henry Handel Richardson, 1929, *The Fortunes of Richard Mahony: Ultima Thule*, William Heinemann; 1971, Penguin.

Henry Handel Richardson, 1948, *Myself When Young*, Windmill Press; 1992, Minerva.

Peter Senge, 1992, *The Fifth Discipline*, Random House.

Babette Smith, 2021, *Defiant Voices,* NLA Publishing.

Gustav Stickley, 1909, *Craftsman Homes*; 1979 (facsimile), Dover Publications, New York.

Willliam Thackeray, 1848, *Vanity Fair*.

Xie Lingyun, in John Minford, 2014, *I Ching*, Viking, New York, p. 236.

Glenn Martin's books

Stories/Reflections on experience

The Ten Thousand Things (2010)

Sustenance (2011)

To the Bush and Back to Business (2012)

The Big Story Falls Apart (2014)

The Quilt Approach: A Tasmanian Patchwork (2020)

Long Time Approaching (2023)

Books on ethics and life

Human Values and Ethics in the Workplace (2010)

The Little Book of Ethics: A Human Values Approach (2011)

The Concise Book of Ethics (2012)

A Foundation for Living Ethically (2020)

Future: The Spiritual Story of Humanity (2020)

Books on family history

A Modest Quest (2017)

The Search for Edward Lewis (2018)

They Went to Australia (2019)

No Gold in Melbourne: A Scottish Family in Australia (2021)

All the Rivers Come Together: Tracing Family (2022)

Poetry collections

Flames in the Open (2007)

Love and Armour (2007)

Volume 4: I in the Stream (2017)

Volume 3: That Was Then: The Early Poems Project (2019)

The Way Is Open (2020)

Local histories

Places in the Bush: A History of Kyogle Shire (1988)

The Kyogle Public School Centenary Book (1995)

The author

Glenn Martin lives in Sydney, although he lived in the bush on the far north coast of New South Wales for two decades. He has been a teacher at high schools and tertiary institutions, a manager of community services organisations, and a commentator on management, business ethics, employment law, and training and development. He has been the editor of publications for management and training professionals and an instructional designer for online learning. He is the author of over twenty books.